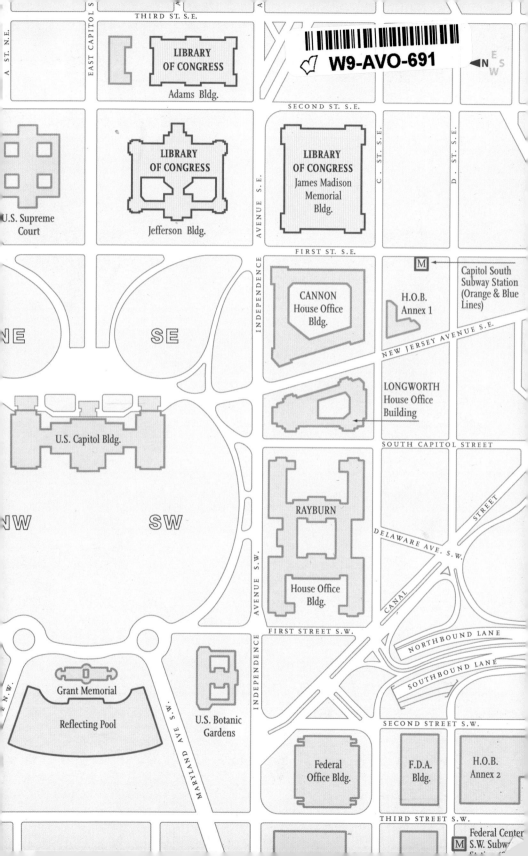

THE LIBRARY OF CONGRESS

The Nation's Library

WASHINGTON, D.C.

THE LIBRARY
OF CONGRESS
The Nation's Library
WASHINGTON, D.C.

*Alan Bisbort, Linda Barrett Osborne,
and Sharon M. Hannon*

*Library of Congress
in association with
Scala Publishers*

For Evelyn Sinclair (1946–2009),
writer and editor, and Elizabeth
Ridgway (1969–2010), national
educational outreach director.

© The Library of Congress, Washington, D.C., 2012

First published in 2000 by
Scala Publishers Limited
Northburgh House
10 Northburgh St
London ECIV OAT
Telephone: +44 (0) 20 7490 9900
www.scalapublishers.com

Revised edition first published in 2012

Published and distributed outside The Library of Congress by
Antique Collectors' Club Limited
6 West 18th Street, Suite 4B
New York, NY 10011
Telephone: 1 212 645 1111
Fax: 1 212 989 3205
Email: sales@antiquecc.com
Library of Congress Cataloging-in-Publication Data
Bisbort, Alan, 1953-
    The nation's library : the Library of Congress, Washington, D.C. /
    by Alan Bisbort, Linda Barrett Osborne, and Sharon Hannon.
        pages cm
    Summary: "A newly up-dated and re-designed celebration and guide
    to the Library of Congress"— Provided by publisher.
    Includes bibliographical references and index.
    ISBN 978-1-85759-672-4 (pbk.)
    1. Library of Congress. I. Osborne, Linda Barrett, 1949-
II. Hannon, Sharon M. III. Title.
    Z733.U6B48 2012
    027.573—dc23
2012005677

Coordinated by W. Ralph Eubanks, Margaret E. Wagner,
and Esme West
Edited by Margaret E. Wagner and Julie Pickard
First edition designed by Anikst Design and Thanh Tung Uong
Printed and bound in China
10 9 8 7 6 5 4 3 2 1

front cover
The dome of the Thomas
Jefferson Building, Library of
Congress, capped by the torch
of knowledge, shares the Capitol
Hill skyline with the white dome
of the United States Capitol.
Photograph by Carol
Highsmith.

inside front cover
Map of Capitol Hill, showing
the three Library of Congress
Buildings.

back cover
A staircase in the Great Hall,
Thomas Jefferson Building.
Photograph by Anne Day.

inside back cover
Schematic diagram of the
Thomas Jefferson Building, by
Doug Stern.

frontispiece
The Commemorative Arch
in the Great Hall, Thomas
Jefferson Building. Photograph
by Anne Day.

right
Volumes on science from
the Rare Book and Special
Collections Division.

Contents

Foreword

The Library of Congress:
A Brief History

Foreword

More than two hundred years ago, the United States was taking its first steps toward becoming a great democratic nation. Born out of revolution and filled with an unyielding independent spirit, the new country was guided by an extraordinary group of people whose ideals had been shaped by the precepts of the Enlightenment— among them, reliance on reason, belief in progress, and profound appreciation of the importance of knowledge in an ever-changing world. "Knowledge will forever govern ignorance," James Madison wrote in 1822. "And a people who mean to be their own governours, must arm themselves with the power which knowledge brings."

In 1800, the Congress of the United States established the Congressional Library to help provide the legislature with the information required to administer this boisterous and expanding land. Under dedicated Librarians of Congress and Library staff, the Library expanded and became not only a resource for Congress but also the national library of the United States and one of the world's greatest intellectual and cultural resources. The initial collection of a few hundred books and three maps has grown into diverse collections numbering over 147 million items—and we continue to acquire thousands more each year.

Treasures humble and sublime are housed within the Library's four main buildings: 4,000-year-old clay tablets concerning the Sumerian economy are cared for here, as are fifteenth-century illuminated manuscripts, sixteenth-century holograph music scores, seventeenth-century scientific treatises, eighteenth-century fine prints and political cartoons, nineteenth-century dime novels and illustrated books, twentieth-century television shows, movies and DVDs, and twenty-first-century electronic publications and "tweets." Reflecting America's history, as well as this country's membership in the community of nations, our collections come from around the world. Researchers from abroad are welcomed here along with the hundreds of thousands of Americans who visit our buildings—their buildings, and their collections— each year. Around the globe, millions more visit us each day via the Internet: as the twenty-first century progresses, more than 19 million primary source items from our collections are accessible on our website, and this electronic resource will continue to expand. Now in our third century of service to Congress, the nation, and the world, the Library of Congress continues to be guided by the belief in the power of knowledge that inspired its creation.

The Nation's Library is a guide to this great and complex institution, outlining its history, collections and current organization, its activities and services. The book's numerous illustrations, drawn from our collections, comprise a celebration of the light human beings have brought to their often shadowed and uncertain world. The Library of Congress has a proud history of preserving and reflecting that light. We invite you to visit us—in person, through this book and our other publications, and via the Internet. We hope you will share this priceless legacy.

James H. Billington
The Librarian of Congress

right, from top to bottom
Thomas Jefferson (1743–1826)
by Jean-Antoine Houdon.
Great Hall, Jefferson Building.
Library of Congress.
Photograph by Reid Baker.

John Adams (1735–1826).
Lithograph after a painting
by John Singleton Copley.
Presidential File, Prints and
Photographs Division.

James Madison (1751–1836).
Watercolor miniature portrait
by Charles Willson Peale. Rare
Book and Special Collections
Division.

The Library of Congress: A Brief History

Thomas Jefferson's name is inextricably linked to the Library of Congress, having been bestowed upon the majestic main building that sits opposite the U.S. Capitol. Jefferson was one of three prime movers for a legislative library after the War of Independence. John Adams and James Madison—for whom the Library's other two buildings are named—were, like Jefferson, devoted bibliophiles who understood the need for a solid intellectual framework on which to build a new nation. Adams, a farmer's son, owned 3,000 books which he studied so that, he wrote, "my sons may have liberty to study mathematics and philosophy . . . in order to give their children a right to study painting, poetry, [and] music." Madison steeped himself in the classics and was the first to suggest, in 1783, that a library be available to members of Congress. Jefferson's love of books is legendary, and the Library owes its very existence to his personal collection and its inventive cataloging scheme. In 1774, both Jefferson and Adams were delegates to the First Continental Congress in Philadelphia—although Jefferson was, in the end, unable to attend. One of the initial acts of this Congress was to secure access to the Library Company of Philadelphia's book holdings.

Thus, the creation of "a Library for Congress" on April 24, 1800, by an act of Congress, was the realization of a shared vision embodying the highest Enlightenment ideals. President John

Adams approved the act, and $5,000 was appropriated for the purchase of "such books as may be necessary," to be housed in the U.S. Capitol in the new District of Columbia. By 1801, the Library had 740 volumes and three maps, all purchased from a London bookseller, Cadell & Davies. In 1802, the collection numbered 964 volumes and nine maps and charts. By 1812, there were 3,000 volumes, covering a range of subjects, including law, literature, history, and agriculture.

The Library was intended to be legislative, a "library for the use of both Houses of Congress." Until moving to a separate building in 1897, it was popularly known as the Congressional Library. Few then would have dreamed that it would become the Nation's Library and one of the world's greatest cultural institutions. In fact, the Library's very existence was threatened soon after it was established when, in August 1814, British troops set the U.S. Capitol ablaze, destroying the Congressional Library—partly in revenge for U.S. troops burning the Parliamentary Library of Canada in 1813.

By 1814, Jefferson had retired to his Virginia home, Monticello, near the town of Charlottesville, after serving two terms as president. Concerned about the Library's destruction, and heavily in debt, he offered to sell his personal library, one of the largest in the nation, though for a fraction of its value. The sale was approved for $23,950, and the 6,487 volumes were brought by ten horse-drawn wagons in May 1815 from Charlottesville to the Library's temporary Washington, D.C. home (until 1818) in Blodgett's Hotel on E Street, N.W.

A cultured man, fluent in Greek, Latin, and French, Jefferson believed that human nature was universal and history provided insight into current events. Of his personal library, he said, "I do not know that it contains any branch of science which Congress would wish to exclude from the collections; there is, in fact, no subject to which a Member of Congress may not have occasion to refer." The acquisition of this library, and adoption of Jefferson's philosophy, together broadened the scope of the Congressional Library. As John Y. Cole, director of the Library's Center for the Book, has noted, "The Jeffersonian concept of universality, the belief that all subjects are important to a Library of the American legislature, is the philosophy and rationale behind the comprehensive collecting policies of today's Library of Congress."

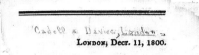

Cadell & Davies, London
LONDON; DECR. 11, 1800.

Gentlemen,

WE were favoured with your joint letter of June 20, inclosing a lift of books for the intended library at Wafhington, and we inftantly fet about executing the order in the beft manner we were able.

Inclofed we tranfmit you the invoice and bill of lading, and we earneftly hope the books will arrive perfectly safe, great care having been taken in packing them. We judged it beft to fend trunks, rather than boxes, which after their arrival would have been of little or no value.

Several of the books fent were only to be procured fecond-handed, and fome of them, from their extreme fcarcity, at very advanced prices.

We have in all cafes fent the beft copies we could obtain, and charged the loweft prices poffible. We annex a lift of a few articles that we have not been able to procure, but, as we firmly truft that the execution of the prefent order will meet your approbation, and that, in that cafe, we may hope to be favoured with your further commands, we fhall continue our fearch for thefe articles, and fend them out with the next parcel.

Meffrs. Baring & Co. paid us the amount of the bill, the inftant it was prefented to them, and we therefore made the ufual deduction of five per cent.

The Cadell & Davies letter of December 11, 1800, preceding the printed invoice which constituted the first printed catalog of the Library of Congress. Manuscript Division.

left
A portion of Thomas Jefferson's personal library on display at the Jefferson Building. Photograph by Michaela McNichol.

The Library's collections and services expanded gradually. The Congressional Library did not evolve into a national institution until after the U.S. Civil War, and the Library of Congress did not become a viable research library until after 1900. While Jefferson, Adams, and Madison had set the tone, Ainsworth Rand Spofford, the sixth Librarian of Congress (1864–97), implemented their acquisitive philosophy, and Herbert Putnam, the eighth Librarian of Congress (1899–1939), shaped the institution into a leader in American librarianship.

A view of the West Front of the Capitol from Pennsylvania Avenue, about 1857. The Library of Congress occupied the space behind the pillars, at the center of the West Front. Prints and Photographs Division.

By 1867, Spofford, a former Cincinnati bookman, had turned the Congressional Library into the nation's largest library, due to the deposit of 40,000 volumes from the Smithsonian Institution and the purchase of an unrivaled trove of Americana, the 62,000-item library of archivist and historian Peter Force. By 1870, Spofford had convinced Congress to revise an old copyright law, the new law requiring anyone claiming copyright on a book to send two copies to the Librarian within ten days of publication.

The former head of the Boston Public Library, Putnam used his four-decade watch to begin services to libraries, such as centralized cataloging, and to acquire world-renowned collections. Also during his tenure, private benefactors were encouraged to underwrite the expense of making the Library of Congress the nation's greatest public cultural institution. Between 1865 and 1939, the combined efforts of these two Librarians saw the collections grow from 70,000 books to 6 million, the staff from seven to 1,100, and annual congressional appropriations for the Library from $300,000 to over $3 million.

To accommodate this transformation, the Library had to expand physically. The Congressional Library, located on the same floor of the Capitol as the House and Senate chambers, was indispensable to government proceedings. But the Library was soon filled floor-to-ceiling with publications, and the clutter spilled over into the attic and along the basement corridors of the Capitol, then to the staircases and first- and second-floor hallways.

By 1880, Spofford was warning of fire (this time caused without British assistance). In fact, two fires had already occurred, in 1825 and 1851, the latter destroying 35,000 volumes, including two-thirds of Jefferson's personal library. Arguing for a safer, separate building, Spofford also played on congressional and national pride in those expansive days of the Gilded Age by touting the advantages of establishing a "temple of learning" that would celebrate the uniqueness of American civilization.

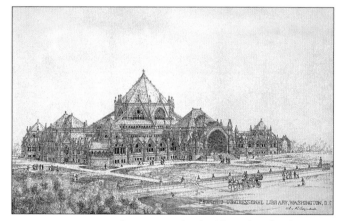

It was not an easy sell, since no other buildings besides the Capitol were on "the Hill" at the time. It took Spofford over twenty-five years to succeed. He proposed the separate Library building in 1871, Congress authorized it in 1886, and the building was opened in 1897. Spofford's conception of the new building was based on the national libraries of Europe, particularly the British Museum Library, and the architects picked up the theme, vowing that "the National Library . . . should be more a museum of literature, science, and art, than strictly taken as a collection of books." It would be "the mecca of the young giant Republic." Spofford pushed for expanded hours of operation and declared that the new building would serve both Congress and the American people. When the building opened, on November 1, 1897, it was called the Library of Congress. Some people referred to it as the new national library.

Ephemera celebrating the opening of the first separate Library of Congress Building: a commemorative plate and postcards picturing the building. Publishing Office.

The opening of its first separate building marked a new era for the Library of Congress. "Twenty years ago . . . the Library was sought for a specific book," Librarian John Russell Young wrote in the Library's 1898 *Annual Report*; "today applicants ask advice as to reading, or request information. It is the policy of the Library to encourage this spirit of inquiry." When Young died in 1899, Herbert Putnam took up his democratic gauntlet, beginning what became an institution-shaping tenure. A Harvard graduate and son of a renowned publisher, Putnam proved equal to the challenge of serving two new constituencies—the public and the library profession. First, he separated the special format collections (e.g. maps, prints, music, manuscripts) from book collections, making them available via new divisions and reading rooms. Second, he focused on the pressing need for centralized cataloging for American librarianship. Finally, he amassed spectacular collections at a pace nearly equal to that of the tireless Spofford.

Putnam incorporated the new Copyright Office into the Library's operation and sought to unify the functions of the new curatorial divisions. Also during his tenure, the Library of Congress Trust Fund Board—the first such body in the federal government—was created to administer the Elizabeth Sprague Coolidge Foundation and all future endowments. (Named for one of the most notable patrons in the history of American music, the Elizabeth Sprague Coolidge Foundation was established at the Library for the promotion and advancement of chamber music through commissions, public concerts, and festivals.)

Continued growth of collections and services required the construction of two additional Library buildings on Capitol Hill. The John Adams Building (1939) opened during Archibald MacLeish's tenure as Librarian, and the James Madison Memorial Building (1980) during Daniel Boorstin's term. Other Library facilities

Librarian of Congress Herbert Putnam, examining one of the three volumes of the Gutenberg Bible. Prints and Photographs Division.

opened over the years include the Division for the Blind and Physically Handicapped, the Performing Arts Library at the John F. Kennedy Center (since closed), several overseas acquisitions offices (in New Delhi, Cairo, Rio de Janeiro, Jakarta, Nairobi, and Islamabad) collecting materials from more than seventy-five countries, storage facilities in Maryland and Virginia—and, in 2007, the Packard Campus for Audio-Visual Conservation in Culpeper, Virginia.

Currently, the Library's 745 miles of shelf space house more than 147 million items, in 470 languages and in formats as old as papyrus and as new as DVDs and "tweets"; the collections expand by approximately ten items every minute. During the two centuries that it has taken to amass these treasures, the institution itself has grown into a Jeffersonian model of intellectual openness and cultural interchange, sharing its collections and services as widely as possible. Among the many inscriptions on the Library walls, two on the second floor of the Jefferson Building's Great Hall may best describe the Library's mission. In the North Corridor, looking toward the U.S. Capitol, is a quotation from Cicero: "Memory is the treasurer and guardian of all things." In the South Corridor, facing the same direction, are the words of Virgil: "The noblest motive is the public good."

"Building" the World's Largest Library

1837   The Library Committee of the U.S. Congress authorizes the first exchange of official publications with foreign nations.

1867   Through the Smithsonian Institution's document exchange system, the Library receives public documents published in foreign countries. The library of Peter Force is purchased for $100,000 and becomes the foundation of the Library's collections of Americana and incunabula (pre-1501 books).

1869   The emperor of China sends 933 volumes to the U.S. government, a donation that forms the nucleus of the Library's Chinese collection.

1870   The U.S. copyright registration and deposit activities are centralized at the Library.

1882   Legislation authorizes the donation of the 40,000-volume library of Washington, D.C., physician Joseph Toner to the Library of Congress. Sen. John Sherman of Ohio calls it "the first instance in the history of this government of the free gift of a large and valuable library to the nation."

1884   A gift of 375 volumes from Sultan Abdul-Hamid II of Turkey establishes the Library's Turkish collection. Each volume is inscribed on the cover, in three languages, "To the national library of the United States of America."

Daguerreotype portrait of former U.S. First Lady Dolley Madison (1768–1849) by Mathew B. Brady, circa 1848. Brady-Handy Collection, Prints and Photographs Division.

1898 The Gardiner Greene Hubbard Collection of engravings, the Library's first major collection of fine prints, is donated by his widow, Gertrude M. Hubbard.

1903 President Theodore Roosevelt orders the transfer, from the Department of State to the Library of Congress, of the records and papers of the Continental Congress and the personal papers of Benjamin Franklin, George Washington, Thomas Jefferson, James Madison, and James Monroe.

1904 The Library purchases a 4,000-volume collection of Indica.

1905 The Library begins a program for copying manuscripts in foreign archives that relate to American history.

1906 The Library purchases the private library of G. V. Yudin of Siberia, which contains over 80,000 volumes of Russian literature.

1907 The Library makes its first large acquisition of Japanese books, 9,000 volumes selected in Japan by Kan-Ichi Asakawa, a Yale University professor.

1908 The Library purchases, from Albert Schatz of Rostock, Germany, his renowned collection of over 12,000 early opera librettos.

1912 A collection of 10,000 items of Hebraica, gathered by Ephraim Deinard, is donated to the Library by Jacob H. Schiff of New York City.

1913 The American Printing House for the Blind begins depositing in the Library of Congress one copy of each embossed book that it produces with federal financial assistance.

1920 Over 300 daguerreotype portraits of prominent Americans made between 1845 and 1853 by the studio of Mathew B. Brady are transferred to the Library from the U.S. Army War College.

1927 Archer M. Huntington of New York City presents the Library of Congress Trust Fund Board with funds to establish an endowment "for the purchase of books relating to Spanish, Portuguese, and South American arts, crafts, literature, and history."

1930 Legislation authorizes the purchase for $1.5 million of the Volbehr Collection of incunabula, which includes one of three surviving perfect vellum copies of the Gutenberg Bible.

1934 The Library becomes the repository for photographs and drawings from the Historic American Buildings Survey

Poster calling for the apprehension of suspected conspirators in Abraham Lincoln's assassination. Broadside Collection, Rare Book and Special Collections Division.

following page
Contents of Lincoln's pockets on the night he was assassinated, and, from the Alfred Whital Stern Collection, a newspaper reporting the assassination. Rare Book and Special Collections Division. Photograph by Roger Foley.

(HABS). Uruguayan poet Emilio Oribe records one of his poems at the Library, inaugurating the Archive of Hispanic Literature on Tape.

1943 The Library announces the gift of a "magnificent collection of rare books and manuscripts" from Lessing J. Rosenwald of Jenkintown, Pennsylvania. The Library purchases more than 9,000 negative plates and photographs by pioneering photographer Arnold Genthe.

1944 The Library assumes custody of the Office of War Information Collection of nearly 300,000 photographs, including the "photo-documentation of America" file organized by Roy E. Stryker in the Farm Security Administration from 1936 to 1942.

1945 The Library purchases the personal library of Sheikh Mahmud al-Imam Mansuri of Cairo, which contains over 5,000 books and manuscripts and greatly strengthens the Arabic collections. The Library establishes a "mission to Europe" to obtain "multiple copies of European publications for the [WWII] period" for distribution to American libraries and research institutions.

1949 The papers of Orville and Wilbur Wright, 30,000 items, including 303 glass-plate negatives documenting their trials with the new flying machines, are donated to the Library.

1950 Chicago businessman Alfred Whital Stern donates to the Library "the most extensive collection of Lincoln literature ever assembled by a private individual."

1954 The Library acquires the Brady-Handy Collection, containing more than 3,000 negatives by Civil War photographer Mathew B. Brady and several thousand plates made by his nephew, Levin C. Handy. The collection is donated by L. C. Handy's daughters.

1964 The Library receives the first installment of the gift of the records of the National Association for the Advancement of Colored People (NAACP), an archive of more than 2.5 million items.

1969 The Library acquires the Charles E. Feinberg Collection of Walt Whitman manuscripts, letters, books, and memorabilia, comprising more than 20,000 items.

1975 The papers of Alexander Graham Bell and his family are donated to the Library.

1978 The Library receives the NBC Radio Collection of 175,000 transcription discs covering 80,000 hours of radio programming from 1926 to 1970.

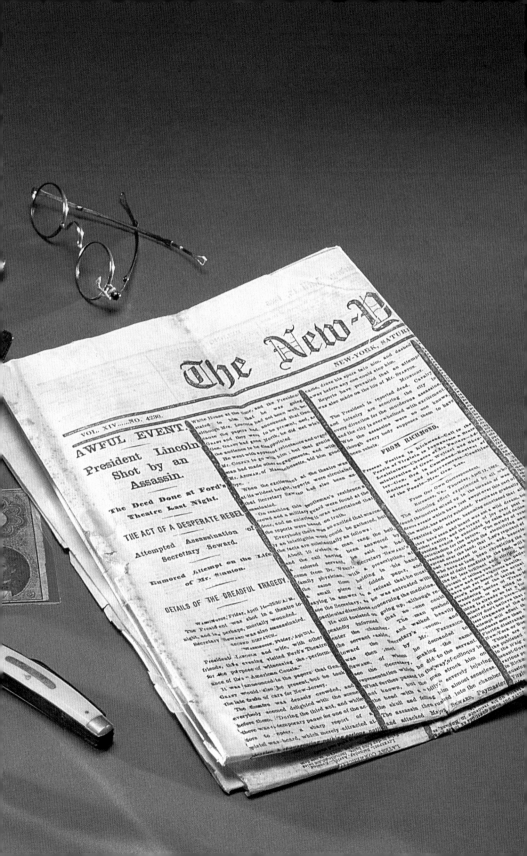

Plywood chairs, sketches of various views. India ink drawing by Ray Eames. Charles and Ray Eames Collection, Prints and Photographs Division.

1988 The Moldenhauer Collection of autograph music manuscripts, letters, and documents, one of the most significant collections of primary source materials in music ever assembled, is donated to the Library, establishing the Hans Moldenhauer Archives. The National Film Preservation Act of 1988 requires the Library to choose and preserve up to twenty-five "culturally, historically, or aesthetically significant" films in a National Film Registry each year.

1989 The James Madison Council is established, an advisory board of business people and philanthropists who contribute ideas, expertise, and funds to support the Library's collections and programs. The Library acquires the Charles and Ray Eames Collection of design, including more than 700,000 papers, drawings, photographs and transparencies, graphics, and motion pictures.

1992 The Library acquires the Irving Berlin Collection of more than 750,000 items, including the musical scores of many of Berlin's most popular compositions. This year, the 100 millionth item is added to the Library's collections.

1993 The Library obtains congressional approval to make its bibliographic data and services available on the Internet.

1999 The Marian S. Carson Collection, comprising more than 10,000 manuscripts, photographs, prints, drawings, books, and broadsides from the Colonial era through the 1876 Centennial celebration, becomes the Library's most significant acquisition of Americana in the twentieth century.

2000 The Library receives 22,000 items each working day, 10,000 of which will become part of the collections. Most are acquired through the Copyright registration process. President William Jefferson Clinton signs legislation creating the Veterans History Project to collect, preserve, and make accessible the personal accounts of American war veterans. Metromedia president John W. Kluge donates $60 million to support an academic center at the Library. The Kluge Center officially opens in May 2003. Congress passes legislation asking the Library of Congress to develop the National Digital Information Infrastructure and Preservation Program (NDIIPP) to preserve digital information, particularly materials that exist only in digital formats.

2001 First Lady Laura Bush cofounds the National Book Festival, which is organized by the Library of Congress's Center for the Book; beginning this year, the festival will be held annually on the National Mall.

2004	Jay Kislak gives the Library of Congress his 4,000-piece collection of rare books, maps, documents, paintings, prints, and artifacts focusing on the early Americas through European contact, exploration, and settlement. The American Folklife Center acquires the Alan Lomax Collection.
2007	Construction of the Packard Campus for Audio-Visual Conservation in Culpeper, Virginia is completed. The facility is financed jointly by philanthropist David Woodley Packard, the Packard Humanities Institute, and appropriations from Congress.
2008	To provide visitors—in the buildings and online—an educational and engaging interface with some of the Library's unparalleled collections, the "Library of Congress Experience" is launched.
2009	In partnership with organizations, museums, and libraries around the world, the Library of Congress unveils the World Digital Library website, containing content from or about all 192 countries belonging to the United Nations Educational, Scientific and Cultural Organization (UNESCO). The Young Readers Center opens, giving children and teens a space in the Jefferson Building devoted exclusively to their reading interests.

One of the unusual items that came to the Library with the Marian S. Carson Collection is this "peepshow book" [Trafalgar Square, London, 184?]. Offering a choice of viewing from three different angles, the book may have been a souvenir from the years soon after Nelson's Column was completed in 1843. Rare Book and Special Collections Division. Photograph by Edward Owen.

The Thomas Jefferson
Building

The John Adams
Building

The James Madison
Memorial Building

The Thomas Jefferson Building

The Thomas Jefferson Building stands atop Capitol Hill, facing west and commanding a view across First Street to the U.S. Capitol. Of the three Library buildings on "the Hill," this ornate Italian Renaissance structure, crowned by a copper dome and the gilded Torch of Learning, is the most recognizable. One of the most beautifully decorated buildings in the United States, it is a dazzling expression of American art, architecture, and self-confidence. Situated on ten acres and two city blocks—bounded by First and Second streets, East Capitol Street and Independence Avenue—the Jefferson Building and its grounds were originally planned as a continuation of the park-like elements of the Mall and an extension of the Capitol Grounds.

Known as the Library of Congress (or Main) Building until June 13, 1980, the Jefferson Building was designed both to house America's

previous page
The illuminated west façade of the Thomas Jefferson Building, facing the U.S. Capitol. Photograph by Carol Highsmith.

left
Interior of the Main Reading Room, Thomas Jefferson Building. Photograph by Jim Higgins.

right
A view of the World's Columbian Exposition, Chicago, 1893. Prints and Photographs Division. Photograph by Frances Benjamin Johnston.

national library and to showcase the art and culture of the growing republic. While the grand scale of the architecture was inspired by the national libraries of England and France, the decoration was American-made. It was modeled on elements in the structures housing the 1893 World's Columbian Exposition in Chicago, an international event that celebrated American cultural achievements.

Many artists who worked on the exposition also worked on the Library of Congress Building, though there was one crucial difference between the projects: the exposition was a private venture, and the Library of Congress Building was the first public building the federal government had authorized to be built, and adorned, on such a massive scale. As Herbert Small, author of the *Handbook*

above
This reproduction of a water-
color by W. Bengough shows
the Library of Congress when
it was located in the Capitol,
with Ainsworth R. Spofford,
Librarian of Congress, stand-
ing on the extreme right, look-
ing at a paper. Prints and
Photographs Division.

right
One of the drawings submitted
in the design competition for
the "proposed Congressional
Library, Washington." This
grand conception, by architect
Alex R. Esty (1826–1881) was
more ornate than the chosen
design. Architecture, Design
and Engineering Collections,
Prints and Photographs
Division.

It was not an easy sell, since no other buildings besides the Capitol were on "the Hill" at the time. It took Spofford over twenty-five years to succeed. He proposed the separate Library building in 1871, Congress authorized it in 1886, and the building was opened in 1897. Spofford's conception of the new building was based on the national libraries of Europe, particularly the British Museum Library, and the architects picked up the theme, vowing that "the National Library . . . should be more a museum of literature, science, and art, than strictly taken as a collection of books." It would be "the mecca of the young giant Republic." Spofford pushed for expanded hours of operation and declared that the new building would serve both Congress and the American people. When the building opened, on November 1, 1897, it was called the Library of Congress. Some people referred to it as the new national library.

The opening of its first separate building marked a new era for the Library of Congress. "Twenty years ago . . . the Library was sought for a specific book," Librarian John Russell Young wrote in the Library's 1898 *Annual Report*; "today applicants ask advice as to reading, or request information. It is the policy of the Library to encourage this spirit of inquiry." When Young died in 1899, Herbert Putnam took up his democratic gauntlet, beginning what became an institution-shaping tenure. A Harvard graduate and son of a renowned publisher, Putnam proved equal to the challenge of serving two new constituencies—the public and the library profession. First, he separated the special format collections (e.g. maps, prints, music, manuscripts) from book collections, making them available via new divisions and reading rooms. Second, he focused on the pressing need for centralized cataloging for American librarianship. Finally, he amassed spectacular collections at a pace nearly equal to that of the tireless Spofford.

Putnam incorporated the new Copyright Office into the Library's operation and sought to unify the functions of the new curatorial divisions. Also during his tenure, the Library of Congress Trust Fund Board—the first such body in the federal government—was created to administer the Elizabeth Sprague Coolidge Foundation and all future endowments. (Named for one of the most notable patrons in the history of American music, the Elizabeth Sprague Coolidge Foundation was established at the Library for the promotion and advancement of chamber music through commissions, public concerts, and festivals.)

Continued growth of collections and services required the construction of two additional Library buildings on Capitol Hill. The John Adams Building (1939) opened during Archibald MacLeish's tenure as Librarian, and the James Madison Memorial Building (1980) during Daniel Boorstin's term. Other Library facilities opened over the years include the Division for the Blind and Physically Handicapped, the Performing Arts Library at the John F. Kennedy Center (since closed), several overseas acquisitions offices (in New Delhi, Cairo, Rio de Janeiro, Jakarta, Nairobi, and Islamabad) collecting materials from more than seventy-five countries, storage facilities in Maryland and Virginia—and, in 2007, the Packard Campus for Audio-Visual Conservation in Culpeper, Virginia.

Librarian of Congress Herbert Putnam, examining one of the three volumes of the Gutenberg Bible. Prints and Photographs Division.

Currently, the Library's 745 miles of shelf space house more than 147 million items, in 470 languages and in formats as old as papyrus and as new as DVDs and "tweets"; the collections expand by approximately ten items every minute. During the two centuries that it has taken to amass these treasures, the institution itself has grown into a Jeffersonian model of intellectual openness and cultural interchange, sharing its collections and services as widely as possible. Among the many inscriptions on the Library walls, two on the second floor of the Jefferson Building's Great Hall may best describe the Library's mission. In the North Corridor, looking toward the U.S. Capitol, is a quotation from Cicero: "Memory is the treasurer and guardian of all things." In the South Corridor, facing the same direction, are the words of Virgil: "The noblest motive is the public good."

"Building" the World's Largest Library

1837   The Library Committee of the U.S. Congress authorizes
the first exchange of official publications with foreign
nations.

1867   Through the Smithsonian Institution's document
exchange system, the Library receives public documents
published in foreign countries. The library of Peter Force is
purchased for $100,000 and becomes the foundation of
the Library's collections of Americana and incunabula
(pre-1501 books).

1869   The emperor of China sends 933 volumes to the U.S. government, a donation that forms the nucleus of the Library's
Chinese collection.

1870   The U.S. copyright registration and deposit activities are
centralized at the Library.

1882   Legislation authorizes the donation of the 40,000-volume
library of Washington, D.C., physician Joseph Toner to the
Library of Congress. Sen. John Sherman of Ohio calls it
"the first instance in the history of this government of the
free gift of a large and valuable library to the nation."

1884   A gift of 375 volumes from Sultan Abdul-Hamid II of
Turkey establishes the Library's Turkish collection. Each
volume is inscribed on the cover, in three languages, "To
the national library of the United States of America."

*Items acquired by the Library
with the Peter Force Collection
include Diego Durán's* Historia
Antigua de la Nueva España
*(1581). Shown is the frontispiece
from Chapter V "Which treats
of how the Aztecs, counseled by
their god, went to seek the prickly
pear cactus and the eagle and
how they found them. And
about the agreement they made
for the building of the city."
Manuscript Division.*

1898	The Gardiner Greene Hubbard Collection of engravings, the Library's first major collection of fine prints, is donated by his widow, Gertrude M. Hubbard.
1903	President Theodore Roosevelt orders the transfer, from the Department of State to the Library of Congress, of the records and papers of the Continental Congress and the personal papers of Benjamin Franklin, George Washington, Thomas Jefferson, James Madison, and James Monroe.
1904	The Library purchases a 4,000-volume collection of Indica.
1905	The Library begins a program for copying manuscripts in foreign archives that relate to American history.
1906	The Library purchases the private library of G. V. Yudin of Siberia, which contains over 80,000 volumes of Russian literature.
1907	The Library makes its first large acquisition of Japanese books, 9,000 volumes selected in Japan by Kan-Ichi Asakawa, a Yale University professor.
1908	The Library purchases, from Albert Schatz of Rostock, Germany, his renowned collection of over 12,000 early opera librettos.
1912	A collection of 10,000 items of Hebraica, gathered by Ephraim Deinard, is donated to the Library by Jacob H. Schiff of New York City.
1913	The American Printing House for the Blind begins depositing in the Library of Congress one copy of each embossed book that it produces with federal financial assistance.
1920	Over 300 daguerreotype portraits of prominent Americans made between 1845 and 1853 by the studio of Mathew B. Brady are transferred to the Library from the U.S. Army War College.
1927	Archer M. Huntington of New York City presents the Library of Congress Trust Fund Board with funds to establish an endowment "for the purchase of books relating to Spanish, Portuguese, and South American arts, crafts, literature, and history."
1930	Legislation authorizes the purchase for $1.5 million of the Volbehr Collection of incunabula, which includes one of three surviving perfect vellum copies of the Gutenberg Bible.
1934	The Library becomes the repository for photographs and drawings from the Historic American Buildings Survey

Daguerreotype portrait of former U.S. First Lady Dolley Madison (1768–1849) by Mathew B. Brady, circa 1848. Brady-Handy Collection, Prints and Photographs Division.

(HABS). Uruguayan poet Emilio Oribe records one of his poems at the Library, inaugurating the Archive of Hispanic Literature on Tape.

War Department, Washington, April 20, 1865,

$100,000 REWARD!

THE MURDERER

Of our late beloved President, Abraham Lincoln,

IS STILL AT LARGE.

$50,000 REWARD

$25,000 REWARD

$25,000 REWARD

Poster calling for the apprehension of suspected conspirators in Abraham Lincoln's assassination. Broadside Collection, Rare Book and Special Collections Division.

following page
Contents of Lincoln's pockets on the night he was assassinated, and, from the Alfred Whital Stern Collection, a newspaper reporting the assassination. Rare Book and Special Collections Division. Photograph by Roger Foley.

1943 The Library announces the gift of a "magnificent collection of rare books and manuscripts" from Lessing J. Rosenwald of Jenkintown, Pennsylvania. The Library purchases more than 9,000 negative plates and photographs by pioneering photographer Arnold Genthe.

1944 The Library assumes custody of the Office of War Information Collection of nearly 300,000 photographs, including the "photo-documentation of America" file organized by Roy E. Stryker in the Farm Security Administration from 1936 to 1942.

1945 The Library purchases the personal library of Sheikh Mahmud al-Imam Mansuri of Cairo, which contains over 5,000 books and manuscripts and greatly strengthens the Arabic collections. The Library establishes a "mission to Europe" to obtain "multiple copies of European publications for the [WWII] period" for distribution to American libraries and research institutions.

1949 The papers of Orville and Wilbur Wright, 30,000 items, including 303 glass-plate negatives documenting their trials with the new flying machines, are donated to the Library.

1950 Chicago businessman Alfred Whital Stern donates to the Library "the most extensive collection of Lincoln literature ever assembled by a private individual."

1954 The Library acquires the Brady-Handy Collection, containing more than 3,000 negatives by Civil War photographer Mathew B. Brady and several thousand plates made by his nephew, Levin C. Handy. The collection is donated by L. C. Handy's daughters.

1964 The Library receives the first installment of the gift of the records of the National Association for the Advancement of Colored People (NAACP), an archive of more than 2.5 million items.

1969 The Library acquires the Charles E. Feinberg Collection of Walt Whitman manuscripts, letters, books, and memorabilia, comprising more than 20,000 items.

1975 The papers of Alexander Graham Bell and his family are donated to the Library.

1978 The Library receives the NBC Radio Collection of 175,000 transcription discs covering 80,000 hours of radio programming from 1926 to 1970.

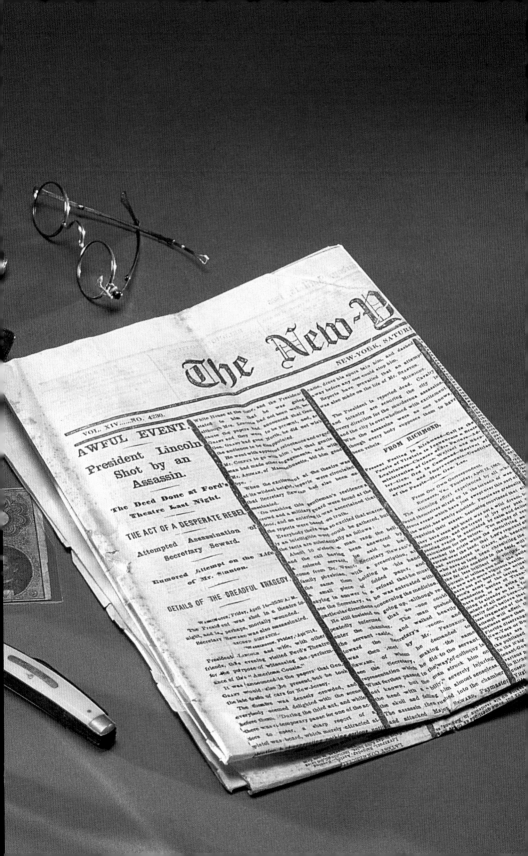

Plywood chairs, sketches of various views. India ink drawing by Ray Eames. Charles and Ray Eames Collection, Prints and Photographs Division.

1988 The Moldenhauer Collection of autograph music manuscripts, letters, and documents, one of the most significant collections of primary source materials in music ever assembled, is donated to the Library, establishing the Hans Moldenhauer Archives. The National Film Preservation Act of 1988 requires the Library to choose and preserve up to twenty-five "culturally, historically, or aesthetically significant" films in a National Film Registry each year.

1989 The James Madison Council is established, an advisory board of business people and philanthropists who contribute ideas, expertise, and funds to support the Library's collections and programs. The Library acquires the Charles and Ray Eames Collection of design, including more than 700,000 papers, drawings, photographs and transparencies, graphics, and motion pictures.

1992 The Library acquires the Irving Berlin Collection of more than 750,000 items, including the musical scores of many of Berlin's most popular compositions. This year, the 100 millionth item is added to the Library's collections.

1993 The Library obtains congressional approval to make its bibliographic data and services available on the Internet.

1999 The Marian S. Carson Collection, comprising more than 10,000 manuscripts, photographs, prints, drawings, books, and broadsides from the Colonial era through the 1876 Centennial celebration, becomes the Library's most significant acquisition of Americana in the twentieth century.

2000 The Library receives 22,000 items each working day, 10,000 of which will become part of the collections. Most are acquired through the Copyright registration process. President William Jefferson Clinton signs legislation creating the Veterans History Project to collect, preserve, and make accessible the personal accounts of American war veterans. Metromedia president John W. Kluge donates $60 million to support an academic center at the Library. The Kluge Center officially opens in May 2003. Congress passes legislation asking the Library of Congress to develop the National Digital Information Infrastructure and Preservation Program (NDIIPP) to preserve digital information, particularly materials that exist only in digital formats.

2001 First Lady Laura Bush cofounds the National Book Festival, which is organized by the Library of Congress's Center for the Book; beginning this year, the festival will be held annually on the National Mall.

2004   Jay Kislak gives the Library of Congress his 4,000-piece collection of rare books, maps, documents, paintings, prints, and artifacts focusing on the early Americas through European contact, exploration, and settlement. The American Folklife Center acquires the Alan Lomax Collection.

2007   Construction of the Packard Campus for Audio-Visual Conservation in Culpeper, Virginia is completed. The facility is financed jointly by philanthropist David Woodley Packard, the Packard Humanities Institute, and appropriations from Congress.

2008   To provide visitors—in the buildings and online—an educational and engaging interface with some of the Library's unparalleled collections, the "Library of Congress Experience" is launched.

2009   In partnership with organizations, museums, and libraries around the world, the Library of Congress unveils the World Digital Library website, containing content from or about all 192 countries belonging to the United Nations Educational, Scientific and Cultural Organization (UNESCO). The Young Readers Center opens, giving children and teens a space in the Jefferson Building devoted exclusively to their reading interests.

One of the unusual items that came to the Library with the Marian S. Carson Collection is this "peepshow book" [Trafalgar Square, London, 184?]. Offering a choice of viewing from three different angles, the book may have been a souvenir from the years soon after Nelson's Column was completed in 1843. Rare Book and Special Collections Division. Photograph by Edward Owen.

The Thomas Jefferson
Building

The John Adams
Building

The James Madison
Memorial Building

The Thomas Jefferson Building

The Thomas Jefferson Building stands atop Capitol Hill, facing west and commanding a view across First Street to the U.S. Capitol. Of the three Library buildings on "the Hill," this ornate Italian Renaissance structure, crowned by a copper dome and the gilded Torch of Learning, is the most recognizable. One of the most beautifully decorated buildings in the United States, it is a dazzling expression of American art, architecture, and self-confidence. Situated on ten acres and two city blocks—bounded by First and Second streets, East Capitol Street and Independence Avenue—the Jefferson Building and its grounds were originally planned as a continuation of the park-like elements of the Mall and an extension of the Capitol Grounds.

Known as the Library of Congress (or Main) Building until June 13, 1980, the Jefferson Building was designed both to house America's

previous page
The illuminated west façade of the Thomas Jefferson Building, facing the U.S. Capitol. Photograph by Carol Highsmith.

left
Interior of the Main Reading Room, Thomas Jefferson Building. Photograph by Jim Higgins.

right
A view of the World's Columbian Exposition, Chicago, 1893. Prints and Photographs Division. Photograph by Frances Benjamin Johnston.

national library and to showcase the art and culture of the growing republic. While the grand scale of the architecture was inspired by the national libraries of England and France, the decoration was American-made. It was modeled on elements in the structures housing the 1893 World's Columbian Exposition in Chicago, an international event that celebrated American cultural achievements.

Fort Meade

Where are all of the books? In addition to the millions shelved in its three main buildings on Capitol Hill, the Library of Congress houses millions of less-frequently used items in its high-density storage facilities at Fort Meade in Maryland. Modules 1 and 2 house 4 million books and bound periodicals, while modules 3 and 4, completed in 2009, hold 33 million items including manuscripts, prints, drawings, photographs, posters, music sheets, maps, and items from the American Folklife Center collections. With temperatures held at a steady 50 degrees Fahrenheit and 30 percent relative humidity, the storage modules are expected to increase the life expectancy of paper-based collections by a factor of five. Four cold storage rooms, built to last 200 years, maintain temperatures between 25 and 35 degrees Fahrenheit to protect more than 400,000 microfilm masters, photographs, and other items in danger of deteriorating in warmer conditions. Sodium vapor lighting is used inside the storage area to eliminate harmful ultraviolet rays, and new acquisitions are quarantined in an isolation room until they are determined to be insect-free. The Library takes these precautions to help it achieve its mission to safeguard these materials for future generations. Daily deliveries bring requested materials from Fort Meade to researchers waiting for them in the reading rooms on Capitol Hill.

Many artists who worked on the exposition also worked on the Library of Congress Building, though there was one crucial difference between the projects: the exposition was a private venture, and the Library of Congress Building was the first public building the federal government had authorized to be built, and adorned, on such a massive scale. As Herbert Small, author of the *Handbook*

one stands at a back-breaking height above the floor, the dome . . . reaches far above, while below, the dark surfaces of hundreds of desks, in concentric broken circles, gleam with the shaded lights of intent readers. Even the brashest tourist speaks in a whisper."

The Main Reading Room

The outstanding features of the Main Reading Room (LJ-100) include the domed ceiling; eight symbolic statues (made of plaster and toned ivory white) set atop the room's eight marble support columns, each with a corresponding inscription; sixteen bronze statues (each embodying a field of knowledge); paintings by Edwin Howland Blashfield along the rim of the dome (and inside the dome's lantern, 160 feet from the floor, is a work representing Human Understanding lifting the veil of ignorance from her eyes); John Flanagan's rotunda clock with the life-size bronze of Father Time; and the forty-eight state seals distributed among the eight semicircular stained-glass windows.

This magnificent room is the primary entrance into the Library's research collections and the principal reading room for the social sciences and humanities. The room houses 70,000 reference books; 226 desks for readers as well as 700 study shelves where a limited number of books may be stored for extended use; and computer workstations in six of the eight alcoves that surround the readers' desks and the Central Desk. The Main Card Catalog, still useful for historical in-depth research, is accessible behind one of the alcoves.

Readers and researchers enter via the southeast ground-floor entrance of the Jefferson Building or via the tunnel from the Madison or Adams Buildings. A Reader Registration Card is required (see Appendix I, "Using the Library," page 146).

The Computer Catalog Center (LJ-139), comprising fifty-eight research stations, is on the east side of the reference area. The Microform Reading Room (LJ-139B), down the hall, provides access to the general microform collection of the Library of Congress. (Other specialized reading rooms, such as the Law, Newspaper, and Manuscript reading rooms, also contain microform collections.)

The General Collections

The core of the Library's holdings of books, monographs, pamphlets, and bound serials is the General Collections, millions of volumes filling twelve levels of stacks in the Jefferson Building and twelve levels of stacks in the Adams Building. Many of the books in the General Collections were acquired through copyright deposit, though some came through gift, exchange, or purchase; they

occupy 257 of the Library's 745 miles of bookshelves (the collections of individual Library divisions occupy the balance of the space). Because 10,000 items are added to the Library's collections daily, space is so precious that some bookshelves in the General Collections' stacks now contain two rows of books, one behind the other.

For security reasons, the General Collections' book stacks, like all storage areas for Library collections, are closed to the public. Requested volumes are retrieved by Library staff and delivered to the appropriate reading room.

Items from the General Collections include a number of foreign-language editions of the hallmark American novel Uncle Tom's Cabin *(above) and many bound periodicals. One of the volumes of* Collier's *magazine back issues includes this number (right), published April 22, 1911.*

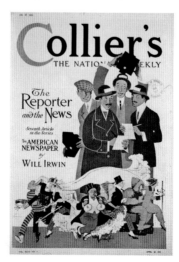

Half the Library's book and serial collections are in languages other than English. Some 470 languages are represented.

The Library's General Collections contain the world's largest historical collection of U.S. telephone criss-cross (phone number and address) and city directories; 8,000 volumes are acquired each year. The General Collections also include historical foreign telephone books and city directories (1,500 received annually from over 100 countries).

African and Middle Eastern Division

The African and Middle Eastern Division Reading Room (LJ-220) is the primary public access point for this division's collections—which include materials in vernacular scripts such as Amharic, Arabic, Armenian, Georgian, Hebrew, Persian, Turkish, and Yiddish. Covering over seventy countries and regions, from Morocco to Southern Africa to the Central Asian republics of the former Soviet Union, the division's three sections—African,

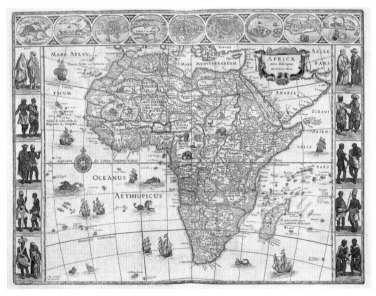

"Africae," from Joan Blaeu, Atlas Maior, 1662–65. Geography and Map Division.

Hebraic, and Near East—offer in-depth reference assistance and produce guides to the Library's rich and varied collections of related materials.

The *African Section* is the focal point of the Library's reference and bibliographic activities on sub-Saharan Africa, which excludes the North African countries of Algeria, Egypt, Libya, Morocco, and Tunisia. The Library's Africana collections encompass every major

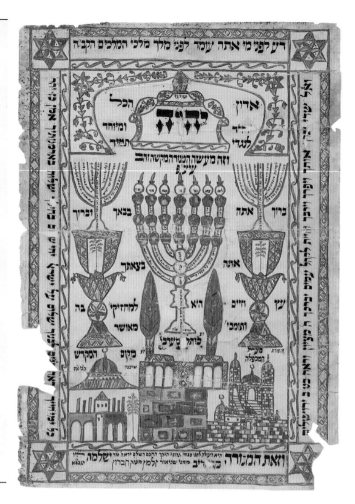

Shivviti Plaques, such as this one dating from the late nineteenth century, were generally decorated with biblical verses forming a menorah (seven-branch candelabrum) and were used in the synagogue and home. This one was created by the itinerant charity emissary from Hebron, Shneur Zalman Mendelowitz. Hebraic Section.

field of study except technical agriculture and clinical medicine, more comprehensive collections of which are found at the National Agricultural Library and the National Library of Medicine.

The *Hebraic Section* is one of the world's foremost centers for the study of Hebrew and Yiddish materials. Established in 1914, the Hebraic Section now holds substantial materials of research value in Hebrew and related languages. Holdings are especially strong in the Bible and rabbinics, liturgy, Hebrew language and literature, responsa (written decisions from rabbinical authorities), and Jewish history. Extensive collections of printed editions of Passover haggadot have been assembled, and the section holds a comprehensive collection of Holocaust memorial volumes.

Established in 1945, the *Near East Section* covers the Arab World, Turkey, Iran, Central Asia, and the Caucasus Republics of Armenia, Georgia, and Azerbaijan. The collections include works in over thirty-eight languages of the region and are, in some cases, the largest in

This rendering of a passage from the Koran, "The Darkening," in Kufic script on vellum probably dates from the ninth century. Near East Section.

"Filban" (elephant driver). Color plate from a nineteenth-century Persian Manuscript, Kitab-i tashrih al-aqvam. Rosenwald Collection, Rare Book and Special Collections Division.

the United States. Priceless manuscripts in Arabic, Persian, Turkish, and Armenian, along with early and rare monographic imprints, long runs of newspapers and serials, and collections of ephemera form the nucleus of a major repository on the Near East.

A watercolor rendering of a rosette from the inside trimming of the mausoleum of Emir Abu-Tengi in Samarkand. From Turkestanskii Al'bom, circa 1880s. Prints and Photographs Division.

American Folklife Center

The United States Congress created the American Folklife Center
in 1976 to "preserve and present American folklife." The center
encompasses the Library's Archive of Folk Culture, which was
founded in 1928 as a repository for American folk music—essen-
tially America's first national archive of traditional life, and one of
the oldest and largest in the world. Today, the American Folklife
Center's multi-format ethnographic collections—which include the
unique Alan Lomax collections—are diverse and international and
include photographs, manuscripts, audio recordings, and moving
images. The Folklife Reading Room of the American Folklife Center
(LJ-G53) is the researchers' access point. Noteworthy collections
include field recordings of music and folklore from rural and urban
areas, interviews with former slaves, record-
ings associated with multiple projects of the
Depression-era Works Progress
Administration (WPA), and field recordings
of North American Indian music dating
from the 1890s to the present day.

With *more than 3 million items, the Archive of
Folk Culture in the American Folklife Center is
the largest repository of traditional cultural documentation in the United States and among the
largest in the world.*

American *Folklife Center collections include the
world's earliest ethnographic field recordings.*

Congress created the Veterans History Project (VHP) in 2000 to collect, preserve, and make accessible the personal stories of American war veterans so that future generations can hear directly from them and better understand the realities of war. A project of the American Folklife Center, VHP collects first-hand accounts (either audio or videotapes or written recollections) of American veterans who served in U.S. conflicts from World War I to the present. United States citizen civilians who were actively involved in supporting war efforts (such as war industry workers, USO workers, flight instructors, and medical volunteers) are also invited to share their memories. Along with the veterans' memoirs, the VHP collects first-hand letters, photographs, drawings, official military documents, and journals or diaries.

Interviewers are essential to preserving the legacy of America's veterans, so the VHP relies on its partners—people who volunteer to record veterans' personal stories—to accomplish its mission. The VHP web page provides resources, guidelines, and tips to help volunteers record the stories of wartime veterans and offers ideas about setting up community and media events to honor veterans' service.

To date, almost 70,000 individual collections have been recorded and preserved through the VHP. About 10 percent of those have been digitized and are accessible through the VHP's web page, which also features selected stories from the archive.

Asian Division

Established in 1869 with the gift of 933 volumes by the emperor of China to the U.S. government, the Library's Asian collections now comprise more than 2.8 million books, periodicals, newspapers, manuscripts, and electronic media from China, Japan, Korea, Mongolia, Tibet, the South Asian subcontinent and Southeast Asia; the collections span the humanities, social sciences, and natural and applied sciences. The 1,000,000-volume Chinese collection is the largest of its kind outside China; among its core collection of more than 2,000 rare books and manuscripts are 1,500 imprints from the Ming Dynasty (1368–1644) and a Buddhist sutra from 975 A.D. The 1.15 million books and serial volumes in the Japanese collection— likewise constituting the largest such collection outside Japan— includes more than 5,500 rare items from the pre-Meiji Period (before 1868). The collection expanded greatly after World War II, with important historical material added. From 1994 until it closed in 2000, the Japan Documentation Center collected "gray literature" (hard to obtain current materials) from Japan and provided bibliographic access to 5,000 items on its database. (Those materials are now searchable online at http://lcweb2.loc.gov/frd/jdcquery.html.)

Similar materials from China, Hong Kong, and Taiwan were added to the Chinese collection.

The Korean collection, begun in the early 1950s, contains 240,000 items and more than 6,500 periodical titles. The South Asia collection contains 233,000 volumes and includes material from Bangladesh, Bhutan, India, the Maldives, Nepal, Pakistan, and Sri Lanka. The Southeast Asia collection, which was separated from the South Asia collection in 2004, includes materials from Brunei, Burma (Myanmar), Cambodia, East Timor, Indonesia, Laos, Malaysia, the Philippines, Singapore, Thailand, and Vietnam.

The Asian Reading Room (LJ-150) is the gateway to material in all Asian languages and about Asian American Studies, the Asian Diaspora, and the Pacific Islands. Materials written in Asian languages are served in the Asian Reading Room.

A portion of the 1629 Chinese Buddhist folding album of the Diamond Sutra. Asian Division.

The second oldest example of printing in the world—four small scrolls with passages from a Buddhist sutra printed in 770 A.D. —is held in the Asian collections.

The Chinese collection, rich in classical Chinese literature and local and regional gazettes, includes ancient works on Chinese agriculture, botany, and medicine, as well as contemporary Chinese publications.

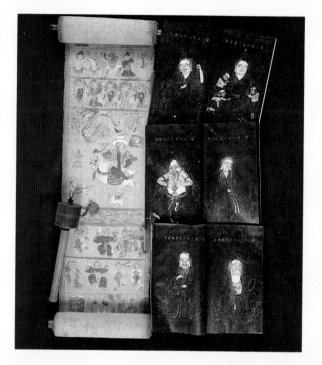

Among the treasures in the Asian Division are, moving from right to left, the depictions of some of the 500 Buddhist worthies, a cloth scroll showing the realms of the Universe, and a Tibetan Buddhist prayer wheel. Asian Division.

The Japanese materials include a collection of traditional mathematics called "wasan" and other classics in religion, history, and literature.

The Korean collection contains materials published in Korean communities outside Korea, including biographies of eighty Soviet-Korean leaders sent to North Korea in the mid-1950s.

Among the most unusual items in the Southeast Asia collection are the writings of the Mindoro–Palawan axis on bamboo strips.

The Tibetan holdings include rare woodblock print redactions of the Tibetan Buddhist canonical literature, Kanjur and Tanjur, as well as complete sets of the Bon Kanjur and Katen.

European Division

The European Division Reading Room (LJ-249) is the primary access point for researchers using the vast collections relating to European countries, including the Russian-speaking areas of Asia. The French, German, and Russian collections alone account for 3.5 million items. Researchers interested in Spain and Portugal should contact the Hispanic Division Reading Room; those interested in the United Kingdom and Ireland should contact the Main Reading Room. The European Division Reading Room holds current, unbound Slavic and Baltic periodicals and recent issues of Western European newspapers and periodicals and collections of pamphlets and "gray literature" (hard to obtain current materials). It also holds microfilmed newspapers from Slavic and Baltic countries.

European materials are found in many Library of Congress divisions. This depiction of the Church of Vassili Blagennoi in Moscow is one of sixty hand-colored plates in Excursions Daguerriennes: Vues et Monuments les plus Remarquables du Globe *(Daguerrean Excursions: The World's Most Remarkable Scenes and Monuments) (Paris, 1842), housed in the Prints and Photographs Division.*

The *Library* holds the largest collection of Russian-language materials in the United States and the largest outside of Russia (750,000 items).

Approximately 50 percent of the Library's rare books are of European origin.

Each year the Library acquires tens of thousands of volumes from Europe: 15,000 from Germany, Austria, and Switzerland; 10,000 from France; 2,000 from Hungary; and 1,500 from the Czech Republic and Slovakia.

Library of Congress holdings of books and other materials from almost all European countries are larger than anywhere in the world outside the countries themselves.

above

Boethius's De Consolatione Philosophiae *(Ghent, 1485) has text in Dutch and Latin, commentary in Dutch, illuminated initials and borders and, at the beginning of each of the five books, miniatures by a Flemish artist, possibly the Master of Edward IV. Rosenwald Collection, Rare Book and Special Collections Division.*

right

The name "America" was first used in Martin Waldseemüller's book, Cosmographiae introductio *(St. Die, 1507), and its accompanying world map (not shown). Thacher Collection, Rare Book and Special Collections Division.*

COSMOGRAPHIAE

Capadociam/Pamphiliam/Lidiam/Ciliciã/Armenias maiorẽ & minorẽ.Colchiden/Hircaniam/Hiberiam/Albaniã:et preterea mᶜtas quas singilatim enumerare longa mora esset.Ita dicta ab eius nominis regina.

Nũc vo & hẽ partes sunt latius lustratæ/& alia quarta pars per Americũ Vesputiũ(vt in sequentibus audietur)inuenta est/quã non video cur quis iure vetet ab Americo inuentore sagacis ingenij vi ro Amerigen quasi Americi terrã/siue Americam dicendã:cũ & Europa & Asia a mulieribus sua sortita sint nomina.Eius situ & gentis mores ex bis bi nis Americi nauigationibus quæ sequũt liquide intelligi datur.

Hunc in modũ terra iam quadripartita cognos= ciẽt sunt tres primæ partes cõtinentes/quarta est insula:cũ omni quaqꝫ mari circũdata conspiciã.Et licet mare vnũ sit quẽadmodũ et ipsa tellus/multis tamen sinibus distinctũ/& innumeris repletum insulis varia sibi noĩa assumit:quæ et in Cosmogra phiæ tabulis conspiciũt/& Priscianus in tralatione Dionisij talibus enumerat versibus.

Circuit Oceani gurges tamen vndiqꝫ vastus
Qui quis vnus sit plurima nomina sumit.
Finibus Hesperijs Athlanticus ille vocatur
At Boreæ qua gens furit Armiaspa sub armis
Dicit ille piger necnõ Satur.ide Mortuus est alijs:

Amerīca

Priscianus

Hispanic Division

Dedicated in 1939, the Hispanic Division Reading Room (LJ-240) occupies the second-floor Southeast Gallery. Designed by Paul Philippe Cret, who designed the Folger Shakespeare Library (across Second Street), the entrance is dominated by four colorful murals by Brazilian artist Candido Portinari. Completed between October 1941 and January 12, 1942, the murals focus on central themes in the past 500-year experience of human contact in the Americas: exploration and discovery (*Discovery of the Land*); taming the environment (*Entry into the Forest*); acculturation and cross-cultural fertilization (*Teaching of the Indians*); and exploitation of natural resources (*Mining of Gold*). The reading room is the primary access point for research into the Caribbean, Latin America, Spain, and Portugal; the indigenous cultures of those areas; and peoples throughout the world historically influenced by Luso-Hispanic heritage, including Latinos in the United States and peoples of Portuguese or Spanish heritage in Africa, Asia, and Oceania. Luso-Hispanic, Iberian, and Caribbean materials can be accessed through the Hispanic Division or through the Main Reading Room.

Four murals by Brazilian artist Candido Portinari decorate the Hispanic Division Reading Room; at left is Discovery of the Land.

The Library's Iberian, Latin American, and Caribbean collections, comprising 10 million items (books, journals, newspapers, maps, manuscripts, photographs, posters, recordings, sheet music, and other materials) are the world's largest.

Since 1943, the Library, through the Hispanic Division, has developed the Archive of Hispanic Literature on Tape. The Archive contains the recordings or videotapes of over 660 authors reading from their own works; eight of those authors have been awarded the Nobel Prize in Literature.

The Collection of Spanish Plays comprises over 8,100 Spanish plays published in the late nineteenth and early twentieth centuries, principally in Madrid and Barcelona. The collection, received from the Hispanic Society of America in 1938, is now on microfilm.

The Archive of Hispanic Culture, a photographic reference collection for the study of Latin American art and architecture, is not housed in the Hispanic Division proper, but in the Prints and Photographs Division.

The Archive of Folk Culture in the American Folklife Center contains recordings of Mexican indigenous and European music, as well as music from Brazil, Chile, Colombia, Cuba, Guatemala, Haiti, Jamaica, Panama, Peru, Puerto Rico, Surinam, Trinidad, and Luso-Hispanics in the United States.

Calendar Wheel. Plate number 5 from Los Calendarios Mexicanos *by Mariano Fernandez de Echeverria y Veytia (Mexico, 1907).*

Kislak Collection

In 2004, renowned collectors Jay and Jean Kislak gave the Library of Congress 4,000 rare maps, documents, paintings, prints, and artifacts from the early Americas up through European contact, exploration, and settlement. The materials in the collection date from 1200 B.C. to the early decades of the United States and contain some of the earliest records of the indigenous peoples of the Americas. They include superb objects from the discovery, contact, and colonial periods particularly in Florida, the Caribbean and Mesoamerica. The collection also includes a rare treasure from 1516 prepared by cartographer and cosmographer Martin Waldseemüller, the Carta Marina, the first printed navigational chart of the entire world. Highlights from this special collection are on permanent display in the *Exploring the Americas* exhibition.

Local History and Genealogy Division

The Local History and Genealogy Reading Room (LJ-G42) serves one of the world's premier collections of U.S. and foreign genealogical and local historical publications. The collection began in 1815, with the acquisition of records from Thomas Jefferson's library. The reading room houses indexes, guides, and other reference works; published genealogies, local histories, and genealogical compendiums. (Primary documents are in the National Archives.) Special catalogs and indexes are generally arranged by family name. In addition to providing information on family histories, the division directs researchers to sources on the history of American communities.

The Library's genealogy holdings include 40,000 family histories and 100,000 local histories, all donated to the collections.

Since the 1700s, British local history societies have produced hundreds of parish registers and other records subsequently acquired by the Library. The collection of local history and genealogical materials on Great Britain and Ireland is so large that it ranks second only to the Library's holdings related to the United States.

"The Steerage." Photograph, 1907, by Alfred Stieglitz. Alfred Stieglitz Collection, Prints and Photographs Division.

The Library suggests that researchers first consult their local public libraries for information on genealogical research.

Although earlier generations of Americans pursuing genealogical research generally focused on ancestors who came before 1783, current interest embraces the wave of immigrants who arrived in the nineteenth and twentieth centuries. A guide to finding Customs Passenger Lists of 1820–1905 and Immigration Passenger Lists of 1883–1945 (both mandated by Congressional Acts regulating passenger vessels) is available in the reading room, while the National Archives holds the records themselves. Local History and Genealogy also assists in finding sources for foreign genealogical research.

Rare Book and Special Collections Division

The Rare Book and Special Collections Reading Room (LJ-239) occupies much of the east side of the Jefferson Building's second floor. The history of printing—a recurring theme in the Jefferson Building—is represented on the bronze doors of this reading room via the printer's marks of ten printers from Europe (left door) and the New World (right door). The unique materials available through this reading room, nearly 800,000 items, include books, broadsides, pamphlets, theater playbills, prints, posters, photographs, and medieval and Renaissance manuscripts. The collections' nucleus is still Thomas Jefferson's library. Other unique holdings include Woodrow Wilson's library and the Harry Houdini, Benjamin Franklin, and Susan B. Anthony Collections (the last, divided between this and the Manuscript Division). Opposite the reading room is the Lessing J. Rosenwald Room, modeled after Mr. Rosenwald's Alverthorpe Gallery in Jenkintown, Pennsylvania, and the repository of the Rosenwald Reference Collection. (The Rosenwald Collection itself, 2,653 illustrated books from the fifteenth through the twentieth centuries, is housed in the Rare Book vaults.)

Two examples of artistic works with scientific purposes held in the Rare Book and Special Collections Division are this "Iris Xiphium" from Pierre-Joseph Redoute's Choix de Plus Belles Fleurs *(1827–33)* and "The Little Owl" from Mark Catesby's The Natural History of Carolina, Florida, and the Bahama Islands *(1771)*.

On Christmas Eve 1851, a fire in the Library's principal room in the Capitol destroyed 35,000 of its 55,000-item collection— including two-thirds of Thomas Jefferson's library. Many of Jefferson's volumes have been replaced, but 900 are still missing. As part of the Library's Bicentennial celebration in 2000, an ongoing worldwide search was started to replace the missing books.

The smallest book in the Library of Congress, Old King Cole, is housed in the Rare Book and Special Collections Division. It is 1/25 by 1/25 inches or about the size of the period at the end of this sentence. The pages can only be turned with a needle. The largest book in the Library is a 5-by-7-foot book featuring color images of Bhutan compiled by students from the Massachusetts Institute of Technology.

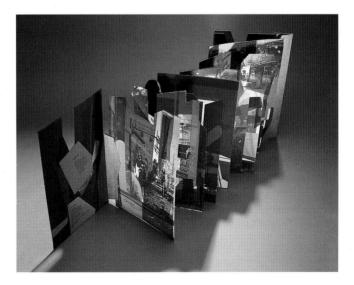

Many modern examples of the book arts are housed in the Rare Book and Special Collections Division. This 1993 collaboration between poet Barbara Luck and illustrator Lois Johnson, Night Street, *was published by the Janus Press. Photograph by Roger Foley.*

The John Adams Building

"**I** cannot live without books," Thomas Jefferson wrote to John Adams in 1815; nor, of course, could the burgeoning Library of Congress. Although Librarian Ainsworth Spofford optimistically predicted that the original building would house collections and programs until 1975, by the late 1920s shrinking storage and office space prompted then Librarian Herbert Putnam to ask Congress for a second building. In 1930, the government appropriated $6,500,000, later increased to $8,226,457, for a functional and efficient book stack "encircled with work spaces" for cataloging and acquisitions specialists.

While the Library of Congress Annex, as it was called until 1976, was both functional and efficient (state-of-the-art conveyor belts and pneumatic tubes were built in to transport books, and catalog cases and table tops pioneered the use of formica, the stain- and burn-proof, cutting-edge plastic), it also came to be recognized as one of the few distinguished Art Deco buildings in Washington, D.C. The architectural firm of Pierson & Wilson, in collaboration with Alexander Trowbridge, designed a structure that would harmonize with its two classically inspired, but stylistically different neighbors: the ornate and monumental Main Building of the Library of Congress (now the Jefferson Building) and the simplified, well-proportioned Folger Shakespeare Library, located next door to the Adams Building. The basic organization and mass of the Annex reflect that of the Jefferson Building, but its spirit and decoration are, like the Folger's, distinctly modern.

The stepped-back upper stories of the Annex's five-story façade mirror the Main Building. The elegant exterior is faced with white Georgia marble and North Carolina pink granite. Vertical bands of windows alternate with planar marble surfaces, and sandblasted friezes adorning the pediment and surrounding doorways are part of its "stripped classical" styling. The "Greco-Deco" ornamentation features variations of the honeysuckle flower, a motif popular in American architecture from the early nineteenth century.

Seven pairs of chased bronze doors bring a touch of exotica to the otherwise restrained building. Lee Lawrie's sculptures of Hermes, Odin, Ogma (credited with inventing the Gaelic alphabet), the gods Itzama (Mayan) and Quetzalcoatl (Aztec), and the Native American Sequoyah personify the history of the written word at the west (Second Street) entrance. The east side (Third Street) celebrates the cultural contributions of three additional gods—Thoth (Egyptian), Nabu (Akkadian), and Brahma (Indian)—as well as Cadmus, the Greek sower of dragon's teeth, the ancient Persian hero Tahmurath, and Ts'ang Chieh, the Chinese patron of writing. The entrance on Independence Avenue (originally intended for the Copyright Office but never used) is marked by a grand, sculpted stairway complete with elaborate lamps and stylized owls. The male figure on the left door represents physical labor; the right door's female figure, intellectual labor.

When the Annex opened in 1939, it contained 180 miles of shelving (compared to 104 miles in the Jefferson Building) able to

Ground Floor (G)

1 East Foyer
2 West Foyer
3 Tunnel to other
  LC buildings at
  "C"ellar Level
4 Main Entrance

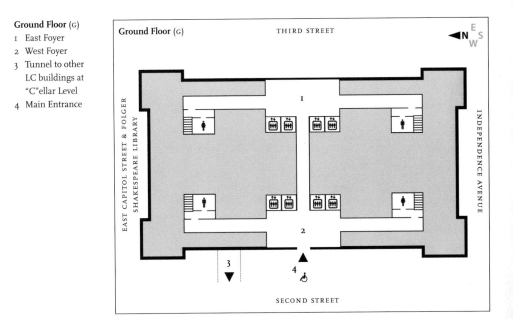

Fifth Floor (5)

1 East Foyer
2 Computer Catalog
  Center (Room LA-526)
3 Book Service Desk
  (Room LA-500)
4 West Foyer
5 Science Reference
  Services
6 Science & Business
  Reading Room
  (Room LA-508)
7 Business Reference
  Services

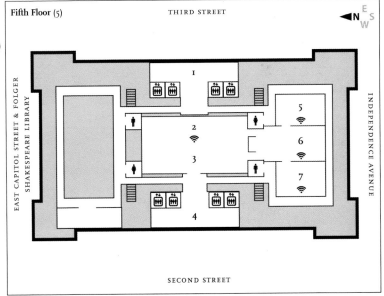

The South Reading Room in the Adams Building, showing Ezra Winter's Jefferson murals. Photograph by Carol Highsmith. Prints and Photographs Division.

hold 10 million books. These shelves were arranged in twelve tiers of stacks reaching from basement to fourth floor, each tier providing thirteen acres of space. Although the storage spaces are closed to the public, visitors can admire the Aztec-inspired lobbies, hallways, fifth-floor reading rooms, and elevators. Walls of American marble are capped by zestful zigzag patterns. Imaginative ornamental plants bloom on doors and walls and above fountains. Lee Lawrie both designed the interior metalwork and supervised production by the Flour City Ornamental Iron Company of Minneapolis.

The building's two fifth-floor reading rooms are enlivened by four 72-foot-long murals by Ezra Winter, who had earlier painted an acclaimed Art Deco mural for Radio City Music Hall in New York. The Science and Business Reference Services Reading Room is dedicated to Thomas Jefferson, for whom the Annex was briefly named,

from 1976 until 1980, when it was renamed the John Adams Building to honor the president who approved the law establishing the Library of Congress. Here, Winter's murals bring to life five passages from Jefferson's writings on the importance of freedom, the virtues of labor, the rights of the living generation, the value of mass education, and the role of the people in democratic government, with an additional lunette of Jefferson himself standing before his beloved home, Monticello. The figures are neither Aztec nor Greco-Deco: they are dressed in the clothing of their time. But the reading room is exuberant with Art Deco details, including handsome bronze lamps on each work table.

In the north reading room (closed to the public as of 2010), two more murals portray Chaucer's pilgrims on their way to Canterbury led by the miller piping them on their journey; the poet himself, with his back toward the observer, rides between the doctor of physic and the lawyer in the midst of the procession. The *Tales'* prologue—"Whan that Aprille with his shoures soote/The droghte of March hath perced to the roote . . ."—is inscribed on the north wall.

The reading rooms in the Adams Building reflect one of the features that won praise for the building: its streamlined interior design, typified by its hallways, said to resemble Pullman cars. Technologically innovative materials included acoustical block, Vitrolite, glass tubing, and formica, for which architects Pierson & Wilson won an award in a national plastics competition. Advertising material for formica declaimed it a way to create "imperishable beauty." In its clean line, decorative ingenuity, and outstanding craftsmanship, the John Adams Building achieved just that.

Federal Research Division

The Library of Congress's fee-based research and analytical service, the Federal Research Division (FRD), provides research and analysis on domestic and international subjects to U.S. government agencies, the government of the District of Columbia, and authorized federal contractors. As expert users of the Library's vast collections, the FRD's researchers and analysts use Library resources, along with other worldwide sources of information, to produce impartial and comprehensive studies on a wide range of social and physical science topics. FRD staff can translate from more than thirty foreign languages into English, and the division offers selected translation services from English into a variety of foreign languages. The FRD provides its clients primary research materials, annotated bibliographies, glossaries, statistical summaries, surveys, databases, studies and reports, and books.

Science, Technology, and Business Division

The Library of Congress has always collected works of science, technology, and business. Thomas Jefferson's library included 500 volumes of natural philosophy, agriculture, chemistry, zoology, and technical arts; eighteenth-century experimental records; and hundreds of works relating to economics and commerce. In 1866, an agreement between Librarian Ainsworth Spofford and Joseph

Henry, Secretary of the Smithsonian Institution, ratified by an act of Congress, transferred the "Smithsonian deposit" to the Library—40,000 scientific books, memoirs, transactions, and periodicals of learned scientific societies, museums, exploring expeditions, and observatories throughout the world. In time, the Library would acquire such treasures and unique resources as first editions of Copernicus, Newton, and Adam Smith's *The Wealth of Nations*; the papers of Samuel Morse, Alexander Graham Bell, the Wright Brothers, and Herman Hollerith, whose company became IBM; primary source materials on Alexander Hamilton and the founding of the First National Bank; and the wartime and postwar reports of the Atomic Energy Commission.

However, a separate Science Division was not established until 1949, following the post-World War II boom in scientific research. In 1998, Science and Technology merged with the Business Reference Section to form the present Science, Technology, and Business Division (LA-508). Together, the collections in these subjects account for nearly 40 percent of the Library's total book and journal holdings.

The first book printed with illustrations of a technical nature, De re militari by Roberto Valturio (1472) includes a number of depictions of fantastic weapons, such as this cannon-shooting, mobile dragon. Rare Book and Special Collections Division.

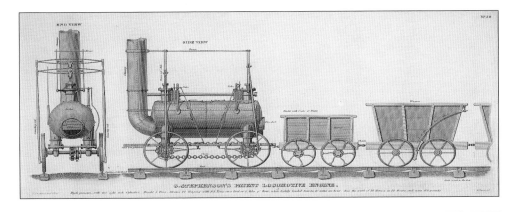

END VIEW   SIDE VIEW

G. STEPHENSON'S PATENT LOCOMOTIVE ENGINE.

Nuclear Reactions and Stability
J. R. Oppenheimer – April 28, 1941

Nuclear Reactions

First carried out by use of bombarding particles from natural radioactive substances.

$N^{14} + He^4 \rightarrow H^1 + O^{17}$ (He = natural α particle)
by Blackett in cloud chamber

$Be^9 + He^4 \rightarrow C^{12} + n$
first source of neutrons - yield small

The γ-rays of thorium C'' (2.62 MeV)

$D + \gamma \rightarrow n + p$ (Chadwick & Goldhaber)

$Be^9 + \gamma \rightarrow n + 2He$ 1.4 binding energy.

In general we will want hi energy particles, especially protons, to get into the nucleus. This can be done at energies less than the coulomb barrier energy $\left(E_c \approx \frac{Z e^2}{(1.2 \times 10^{-13} A^{1/3})}\right)$ because of the wave effects which allow the particles to diffract through the barriers. There are often ample nuclear reactions produced by bombarding particles of energy less than the coulomb barrier.

top

Benjamin Tanner, after William Strickland. C. Stephenson's Patent Locomotive engine. Engraving with watercolor from Strickland, Report on Canals, Railways, Roads, and other Subjects, *made to the Pennsylvania Society for the Promotion of Internal Improvements.* Philadelphia, 1826. *Rare Book and Special Collections Division.*

above

J. Robert Oppenheimer. Nuclear Reactions and Stability. Equations on this page refer to English physicist Patrick M. S. Blackett's cloud chamber experiments of the 1920s and to the 1932 discovery of neutrons—which would prove to be the most useful particles for initiating nuclear reactions. Pen and ink. [California], April 28, 1941. Manuscript Division.

Although clinical medicine materials are housed at the National Library of Medicine, the Library of Congress has more medical books than most medical libraries, as well as collateral materials in such areas as alternative medicine, medicinal plants, and women's health. Likewise, although the National Agricultural Library has the main collection for technical agriculture, the Library of Congress has strong collections on other facets, especially on the economic and social aspects of agriculture.

The Library's technical reports and standards collection is one of the world's largest. Depending on one's definition of a "technical report," the Library houses more than 6 million technical reports on microfilm, CD, and in print, and thousands of standards, some of which are online.

Typical business and economics reference services for Congress and the nation include in-person reference assistance from the 20,000-volume business reference collection and Internet terminals; assistance to entrepreneurs; practical information on everything from raising earthworms to computer repair; company, stock, and bond information for investors; and access to the Library's unique historical book and periodical collections and data sources in business and economics.

The James Madison Memorial Building

"**W**hat spectacle can be more edifying or more seasonable, than that of Liberty & Learning, each leaning on the other for their mutual & surest support?" wrote James Madison in 1822. Madison, to whom the third building of the Library of Congress is dedicated, was the first to suggest that a library be available to members of Congress (the Continental Congress, meeting in 1783 under the Articles of Confederation). He even prepared a list of books "proper for the use of" his colleagues, but his dream was not realized until 1800. After the British burned the original Library of Congress collection during the War of 1812, then-President Madison secured Thomas Jefferson's personal library for the nation. Thus, Madison's belief in "Liberty & Learning" and his role in support of the Library, added to his service as statesman and "Father of the U.S. Constitution," make it fitting that his memorial be a dynamic center of knowledge and culture. Originally planned as separate buildings—a Library annex and a Madison Memorial—the two were combined in 1965, and construction began in 1971.

The need for an additional building became critical in the 1950s, when the shortage of storage and work space was so acute that collections were housed in outlying airplane hangars and truck warehouses and staff were scattered throughout Washington, D.C., Virginia, and Maryland. By 1958—only twenty years after the Adams Building was completed—the information explosion that followed World War II had more than doubled the Library's collections and staff. As Librarian L. Quincy Mumford told a Joint Committee of Congress, "We have reached the place where we are literally bursting at the seams."

The response was to build the largest library structure in the world. Designed by the architectural firm DeWitt, Poor, and Shelton, the Madison Building is a rectangular structure faced in marble and granite, whose columns pay homage to the classical inspiration of the Jefferson Building, and whose simplicity and polished surfaces harmonize with the Adams Building.

Unlike the Jefferson Building, the Madison Building is not a highly ornamented "Temple of the Arts." It is crisply functional, with extensive computer installations and every room wired for television and computer data transmission. The modular interior was planned for maximum flexibility; walls can be moved and rearranged. There is no specific stack area, since all floors are strong enough to support books at any point. Motorized compact shelving holds twice as many books as the same space of conventional shelving, sliding apart to provide access only when needed.

The statue of James Madison, by sculptor Walter K. Hancock, is the central feature in the James Madison Memorial Hall. Photograph by Jim Higgins.

Most visitors enter the building on Independence Avenue, under a four-story bronze relief, *Falling Books*, by Frank Eliscu. After passing through the security checkpoint, immediately to the left is the James Madison Memorial Hall, two stories high and lined with marble and teak; the centerpiece is a 12-foot statue of Madison as a young man, holding volume 83 of the French *Encyclopédie Méthodique*. Walter Hancock carved this work from a 30-ton block of Italian marble, while Constantine L. Seferlis incised eight quotations from Madison on the paneled walls.

Ahead is a spacious lobby area, where small exhibits are sometimes shown; there is an information desk on the left and an atrium at the far side. Down the hallway to the left is the Reader Registration and Research Guidance room (LM-140), the first stop for all those wishing to use the Library's research areas (see page 146).

Divided into four color-coded quadrants housing special collections reading rooms, public service areas, a film theater, and lecture and meeting rooms, the Madison Building also houses the Library's administrative offices, including that of the Librarian of Congress, and the Congressional Research Service, which is dedicated to providing non-partisan, objective research, analysis, and information services to members and committees of Congress.

James Madison Memorial Building (LM)

First Floor (1)

1 Main Entrance
2 Madison Hall
3 Manuscript Reading Room (Room LM-101)
4 Manuscript Division Office (Room LM-102)
5 Atrium
6 Reader Registration & Researcher Guidance (Room LM-140)
7 Newspaper & Current Periodical Reading Room (Room LM-133)
8 Recorded Sound Resource Center
9 Performing Arts Reading Room (Room LM-113)
10 Veterans History Project Info Center (Room LM-109)
11 Human Resources Service Center (Room LM-107)

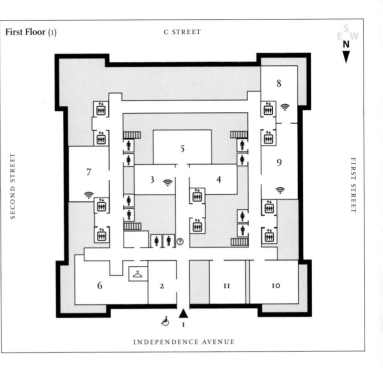

Sixth Floor (6)

1 Mumford Room (Room LM-649)
2 Oval Gallery
3 Madison Cafeteria
4 West Dining Room (Room LM-21)
5 Dining Room A (Room LM-620)
6 Montpelier Room (Room LM-619)
7 Dining Room C (Room LM-619)
8 LC Federal Credit Union

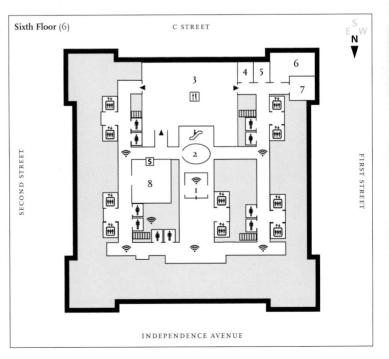

Small exhibitions are open to the public at the entrance of the Performing Arts and Geography and Map reading rooms. Treasures from the Geography and Map Division are also displayed on the sixth floor: two late seventeenth-century globes—one celestial, one terrestrial—designed by Father Vincenzo Maria Coronelli (1650–1718) and made in Venice.

left
Terrestrial and Celestial Globes created by America's first globe maker, James Wilson. The two smaller globes date from circa 1820. The larger, 13-inch globe dates from 1811. Geography and Map Division. Photograph by Roger Foley.

right
The Mediterranean and Western Europe, 1559. Mateo Prunes, Vellum Chart Collection, Geography and Map Division.

Geography and Map Division

The Geography and Map Division (LM-B01) houses the world's largest and most comprehensive cartographic collection. The division was officially organized as the Hall of Maps and Charts in 1897 to serve Congress and federal agencies. But as the first director, Philip Lee Phillips, predicted in 1901, "this collection . . . will in time be of great value, not only to the cartographer, but also to the historian." The collection includes many treasures: Henricus Hondius' brilliantly colored world map, which first appeared in a 1633 atlas; a manuscript map of the Kingdom of Ethiopia, prepared by the court geographer in Addis Ababa "by order of the Regent" in 1923; powder horn maps from the French and Indian War (1754–63); and a 1543 terrestrial globe housed within a series of eleven interlocking armillary rings produced by German mathematician and geographer Caspar Vopel in Cologne. In 2003, the Library acquired an extremely rare gem for the collection—the only known copy of Martin Waldseemüller's 1507 world map, the first map to include North and South America and the first document to name these new lands "America."

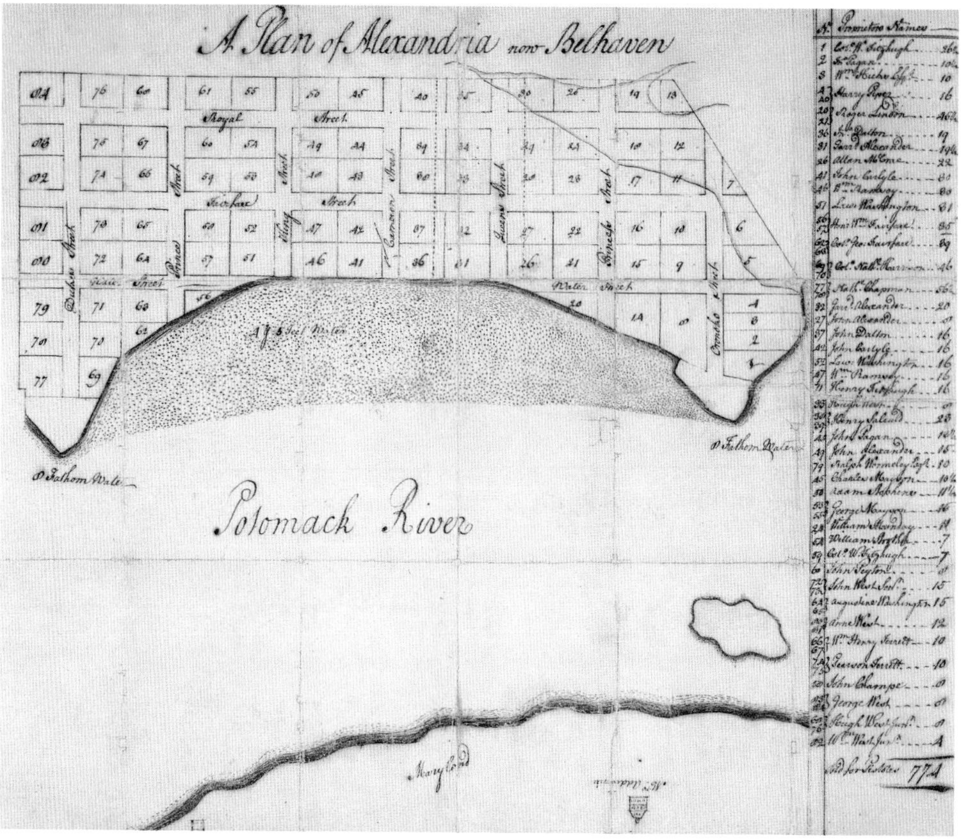

A Plan of Alexandria now Belhaven

Potomack River

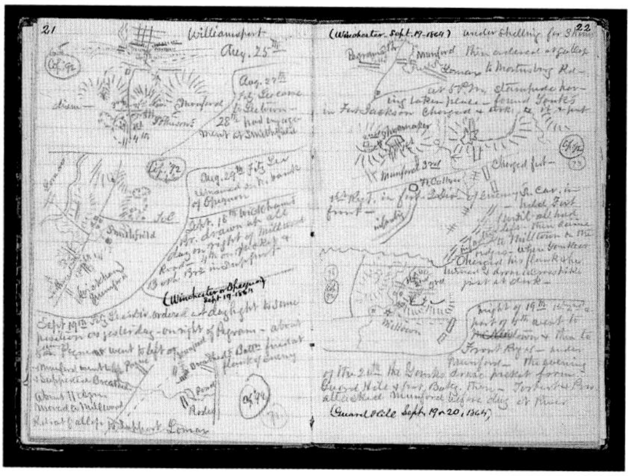

Maryland

Military history is well represented in the Geography and Map collections, including thousands of maps prepared by both Union and Confederate topographical engineers during the American Civil War.

The Library houses 5.3 million maps, 80,000 atlases, 700,000 microfilm images, as well as many globes and terrain models. The Geography and Map Division acquires 60,000 to 80,000 maps and 2,000 atlases per year.

Genealogists and social historians often use the 700,000 large-scale Sanborn fire insurance maps detailing commercial, industrial, and residential properties in 12,000 American cities. Many city blocks have been remapped eight times since the maps first appeared in 1867.

Law Library

When the Library of Congress was established in 1800, works on law comprised nearly one-fifth of its holdings. Thomas Jefferson's library, which re-established the Library in 1815, included 475 law titles in 639 volumes (in Jefferson's now famous classification scheme, "foreign law" encompassed not only continental European works but also laws of U.S. states outside of Virginia). Access to law books was deemed so important to the legislature that in 1816 a move began in the Senate to separate the law collection from the main library, and an act of Congress to this effect was finally passed establishing the Law Library as a distinct department in 1832. The Justices of the Supreme Court, who gained use of the main Library in 1812, were made the administrators of the congressional Law Library, an arrangement that lasted until 1935, when the Supreme Court Building was completed with its own library.

above left

George Washington's plan of Alexandria, Virginia, 1749. Geography and Map Division.

left

Jedediah Hotchkiss (Confederate States of America). Pages from the sketch-book of the Second Corps, Army of Northern Virginia, in engagements of 1864–65. Pen and ink, pencil and watercolor. Hotchkiss Collection, Geography and Map Division.

right

Royal cedula from Emperor Charles V granting Hernando Cortes a coat of arms. March 7, 1525. Edward Stephen Harkness Collection, Manuscript Division.

Today, the Law Library of Congress (LM-201) is the world's largest
law library, holding 2.65 million volumes spanning all periods of
law and covering virtually every jurisdiction in the world. The Law
Library's primary mission is to provide research and legal information to the U.S. Congress as well as to the executive and judicial
branches. The de facto national law library, it is also available to the
public as a law library of last resort. Its staff maintains up-to-date
collections, online and in many other formats and languages, for
many of the world's legal systems, including both primary and sec-
ondary legal sources. The Law Library Rare Book Collection, with
25,000 incunabula, manuscripts, and other material, houses outstanding legal rarities, such as a fourteenth-century miniature edition of the Magna Carta and a velvet-bound fifteenth-century work
on French customary law, Le grande coustumier de Normandie, which
contains several intricate, gilded illuminations.

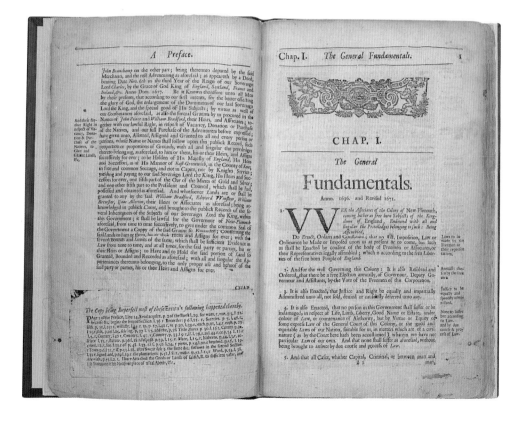

Among the items that came
to the Library of Congress from
the library of the Russian tsars
were illustrated books providing
detailed instructions on the dress
and comportment of Russian
military forces. Several of these
volumes are shown here, on a
background of rare maps from
the Geography and Map
Division. Law Library,
Photograph by Reid Baker.

Each year, some 50,000 volumes, 1,700 reels of microfilm,
75,000 pieces of microfiche, 50,000 serial pieces, and 50,000
official gazettes are added to the Law Library's collections.

The Law Library's collections occupy 59 miles of shelving.

The Law Library's Global Legal Information Network (GLIN)
allows online access to a multinational legal database with
countries contributing information from around the world.

Manuscript Division

It is "the duty of every good citizen," Thomas Jefferson stated, "to use all the opportunities which occur to him, for preserving documents relating to the history of our country." Some of Jefferson's manuscript collection relating to the early history of Virginia and the United States was included in the library he sold to Congress in 1815. The Manuscript Division (LM-101) was one of the departments established in 1897 when the Library moved from the Capitol to its own building. Then, it had 25,000 items; by 2010, it held more than 60 million letters, diaries, notebooks, accounts, logs, scrapbooks, press clippings, photographs, speech drafts, telegrams, and other documents, organized in 11,500 separate collections. Most are personal papers of presidents and congressmen, authors and scientists, explorers and activists. Each holding is unique, many are priceless: Jefferson's Rough Draft of the Declaration of Independence, James Madison's notes on the Constitutional Convention, Alexander Graham Bell's first drawing of the telephone, and the Gettysburg Address in Lincoln's own hand. But the Manuscript Division also preserves the words and experiences of ordinary individuals, including soldiers' correspondence and slave narratives.

One of only twenty-four surviving copies of the first printed Declaration of Independence created on July 4, 1776, by the Philadelphia printer John Dunlap. This was George Washington's personal copy, sent to him on July 6 by the president of the Continental Congress, John Hancock, whose letter is shown on the left. Manuscript Division. Photograph by Roger Foley.

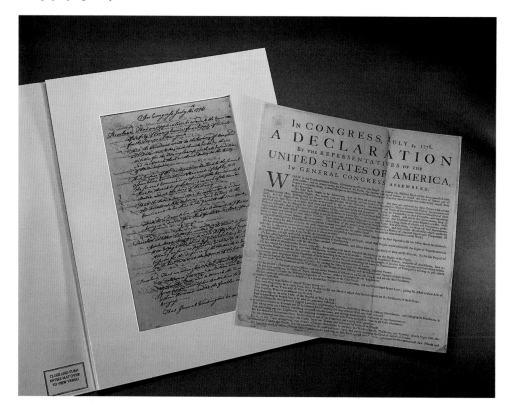

Walt Whitman: "O Captain,
My Captain," with Whitman's
corrections. Manuscript Division.

Ethel Payne (left) and Alice
Dunnigan, the second and first
African American women,
respectively, to be admitted to the
White House press corps.
Payne's many accomplishments
as a print and broadcast jour-
nalist are reflected in the Ethel L.
Payne Papers. Manuscript
Division.

following page
Two pages from The Harriman
Expedition: Chronicles and
Souvenirs, May to August
1899 *compiled during a scien-*
tific expedition along the
Alaskan coast funded and
accompanied by railroad mag-
nate Edward H. Harriman.
Manuscript Division.

The *Library's manuscript holdings are remarkably diverse.*
One random storage aisle contains 261,800 pieces from
Sigmund Freud's files, the Pennell-Whistler Collection, and the
letters and papers of Montgomery Meigs, Daniel Chester French,
Charles Evans Hughes, and Mies van der Rohe.

The *Library holds the papers of twenty-three American presi-*
dents, from George Washington to Calvin Coolidge.

In *1900, the Manuscript Division began assembling one of the*
most comprehensive records of women's experience in the U.S.,
including the papers of those involved in the antislavery, suffrage,
social reform, and labor movements.

Louis Agassiz Fuertes.
Off Cape Elizabeth, Alaska.
July 22nd 99.

To the Golden Crowned Sparrow in Alaska.

Oh minstrel of these barren hills,
  Where twilight hours are long
I would my boyhood's fragrant days
  Had known thy plaintive song.

Had known thy vest of ashen gray,
  Thy coat of black and brown,
The lines of jet upon thy head
Beside thy golden crown

We heard thee in the cold White Pass,
  Where cloud and mountain meet;
Again where foaming glacial tide
  Shone far beneath our feet.

I bask me now on emerald heights,
  To catch thy faintest strain;
But cannot tell if in thy lay
There is more joy or pain.

Motion Picture, Broadcasting and Recorded Sound Division

In 1893, W. K. L. Dickson deposited for copyright, on behalf of the Thomas Edison Company, a series of motion pictures titled *Edison Kinetoscopic Records*, inaugurating the world's first archival motion picture collection. In the following twenty years, thousands of movies were deposited as paper prints—movies contact-printed on paper rolls or strips—since the copyright law did not provide for protection of motion pictures until 1912 (many of these are now included in the division's Paper Print Collection). Thereafter, the Library returned the highly flammable nitrate film to producers, keeping only paper-based materials on the copyright submissions. Only in 1942 did the Library recognize the importance of developing a national research collection of motion pictures and begin keeping selected films and acquiring others through donations. Today the Library houses the largest film collection in the world.

The Library began acquiring television programs in 1949—the first a "Hopalong Cassidy" feature—thus becoming a major tele-

Edison Kinetoscopic Record of a Sneeze
Taken & Copyright by W.K.L.Dickson
Orange N.J. — Jan. 7th 94

left
The Edison Kinetoscopic Record of a Sneeze *is one of a series of short films made in 1894 by W. K. L. Dickson, a young Englishman who was one of Thomas A. Edison's best assistants. The star is Fred Ott, an Edison employee known to his fellow workers for his comic sneezing and other gags. Motion Picture, Broadcasting and Recorded Sound Division.*

right
Ferdinand Joseph "Jelly Roll" Morton (1885–1941), generally acknowledged as jazz's first composer, considered himself the inventor of jazz. He probably wrote this manuscript score of the "Frog-i-More Rag" (Music Division) in 1908. The recording, made some forty years later, and the tinted photograph of Morton are from the Nesuhi Ertegun Collection of Jelly Roll Morton Recordings. Motion Picture, Broadcasting and Recorded Sound Division. Photograph by Roger Foley.

vision archive. Television program acquisition expanded in 1966 to meet the growing demand for research materials. Major television collections held by the division include the NBC Television Collection, National Education Television Programs, and the Public Broadcasting Service Collection. The Motion Picture, Broadcasting and Recorded Sound Division also holds the nation's largest public collection of sound recordings, nearly 3 million items, comprising music of all kinds, radio broadcasts and the spoken word. The collection dates back to the beginning of commercial sound recording over 100 years ago and consists of nearly every audio medium ever used, from wax cylinders to compact discs. Although international in scope, the commercially published sound recordings are predominantly American in origin and contain an outstanding collection of pre-1900 recordings, operatic recordings and extensive holdings of twentieth-century American music of all types. The Library holds 260,000 recordings (on 78 rpm records and LPs) of classic blues and jazz, creating an unparalleled jazz record collection.

The audio collections also include cultural events recorded at the Library: scholarly talks; Music Division Concert Series recordings; and the Library's Archive of Recorded Poetry and Literature and the Archives of Hispanic Literature on Tape, which, together, comprise readings by most major twentieth-century poets from the western hemisphere.

Clarabell the clown, a beloved character on the U.S. television children's show Howdy Doody *(1947–1960), was played in 1949 by NBC staffer Bob Keeshan, who subsequently hosted his own show,* Captain Kangaroo. *Motion Picture, Broadcasting and Recorded Sound Division.*

The Library has major motion picture studio collections from the pre-1951 nitrate era containing original camera negatives and other materials of classic Hollywood features and short films.

The Library's motion picture collection includes ethnographic films of Native Americans, movies originally intended for African American audiences, features and newsreels confiscated at the end of World War II from Germany, Japan, and Italy, and the anthropological films of Margaret Mead.

A notable audio collection is the Emile Berliner Collection comprising disc recordings, scrapbooks, photographs, and laboratory notebooks of the man who created the commercial 78 rpm record.

Among the more than 500,000 radio programs held by the Library are collections donated by radio networks, performers, writers, and producers. The largest are those of the National Broadcasting Company (NBC), the Armed Forces Radio and Television Service (AFRTS), the Office of War Information, the Voice of America, and National Public Radio.

Under the terms of the National Recording Preservation Act of 2000, the Librarian of Congress, with advice from the Library's National Recording Preservation Board, selects twenty-five recordings each year that are "culturally, historically, or aesthetically significant" and are at least ten years old to add to the National Recording Registry. By 2011, the Registry included more than 325 recordings.

PAGANINI.

Packard Campus for Audio-Visual Conservation

The Packard Campus for Audio-Visual Conservation in Culpeper, Virginia, is a $155 million state-of-the-art facility financed jointly by a gift from philanthropist David Woodley Packard and the Packard Humanities Institute and appropriations from Congress. Opened in 2007, the campus gives the Library of Congress a single site at which to acquire, preserve, and provide access to the world's largest and most comprehensive collection of films, television programs, radio broadcasts, and sound recordings.

With more than 90 miles of shelving to store the collections; thirty-five climate-controlled vaults for sound recording, safety film, and videotape; and 124 individual vaults for the more flammable nitrate film, the 45-acre campus now houses more than 6.2 million moving images, sound recordings and related documents. Researchers in the Library's reading rooms on Capitol Hill can access copies of digital files from the Packard Campus. (Films that have not been digitized are sent to Capitol Hill for viewing.)

The Packard Campus also provides preservation services for other public and private sector archives and libraries and shows films and television programs in its 206-seat theater, which is equipped with a projection booth capable of showing everything from nitrate film to modern digital cinema. The theater also features a custom-made organ that provides live music accompaniment for silent movies. Many events are free to the public.

Music Division/Performing Arts Reading Room

The vast holdings of the Music Division (LM-113)—nearly 8 million items and growing—constitute a library-within-a-library of books, music manuscripts, printed scores, rare instruments, and ephemera related to music, theater, dance, and opera over 800 years. What began as thirteen books on music literature and theory

left
Caricature of Niccolo Paganini (1782–1840) by an unknown artist. Whittall Foundation Collection. Music Division.

below and below right
"Le Tango," music from Sports et Divertissements *by Erik Satie (1855–1925), a stubbornly nonconformist composer who delighted in tilting at musical pomposity. This volume of his works includes twenty musical miniatures on various diversions, each accompanied by a color illustration by Charles Martin. The volume was a gift to the Library from Ira Gershwin. Music Division.*

The Music Division houses close to 500 special collections in music, theater, and dance. While some include only a dozen items, others, such as the Irving Berlin Collection, contain over half a million.

George Gershwin's first metronome, Victor Herbert's death mask, a lock of Beethoven's hair, and Paganini's handwritten recipe for ravioli are among the novelties in the division's collections.

One of the world's most extensive collections devoted to the history and performance of a single instrument—the Dayton C. Miller Flute Collection—is housed in the Music Division. Included are 1,600 flutes, a 3,000-volume library, printed music, and pictures.

The Library holds 252 music manuscripts by Franz Liszt and many of his hand-annotated printed scores. Original manuscripts by Bela Bartok and Zoltan Kodaly join autograph scores and correspondence by Johann Sebastian Bach, Alban Berg, Anton Bruckner, Richard Strauss, and Richard Wagner. The Johannes Brahms holdings are the largest outside Vienna.

The achievements and development of American musical theater are celebrated in the Bob Fosse/Gwen Verdon Collection, the Oscar Hammerstein II Collection, the Leonard Bernstein Collection, and the George and Ira Gershwin Collection.

Cover of the sheet music for Irving Berlin's Oh! How I Hate to Get up in the Morning *(1918). Irving Berlin Collection. Music Division*

opposite
Duke Ellington, circa 1947. Photograph by William P. Gottlieb. Gottlieb Collection. Music Division.

from Thomas Jefferson's library grew to 400,000 items (many of them copyright deposits) by the time the Music Division was formed in 1897. Between 1925 and 1935, two benefactors, Elizabeth Sprague Coolidge and Gertrude Clarke Whittall, donated major manuscript collections and created foundations for musical performance and commissioning new works. Thus, the Library is uniquely able to support the creation of new music while adding the original manuscripts to its collections. One example is the score, by Aaron Copland, and the choreography, by Martha Graham, of *Appalachian Spring*, commissioned by the Library and premiered on October 30, 1944, at the Library's Coolidge Auditorium. Other holdings include autograph scores by Beethoven, Mozart, and Prokofiev.

Newspaper and Current Periodical Reading Room/Serial and Government Publications Division

In 1830, Congress instructed Librarian John Silva Meehan to place the latest issues of periodicals on a special table "for the convenience of readers." In 1867, a separate Periodicals Room was established for members of Congress, and three years after the Periodical Division was established in 1897, scholars could use a designated Newspaper–Periodical Room in the new Library Building. Today, the Newspaper and Periodical Reading Room is on the first floor of the Madison Building (LM-133).

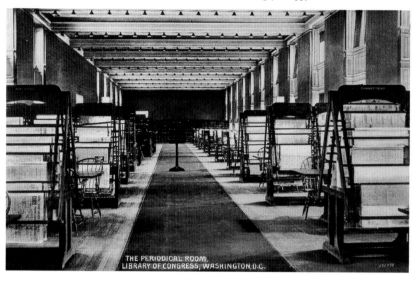

THE PERIODICAL ROOM.
LIBRARY OF CONGRESS, WASHINGTON, D.C.

An early postcard illustration of the Periodical Room in the first Library of Congress Building.

The Library acquires 1,500 current newspapers from around the world and holds 1 million loose issues, 33,000 bound volumes, and 500,000 microfilm reels. It also holds foreign and domestic newspapers back to the seventeenth century, with specialized microfilm copies of early English and American colonial newspapers, early African American newspapers, German and Japanese prisoner-of-war camp newspapers, and the Russian Revolution Newspaper Collection. The Serial and Government Publications Division maintains 70,000 current unbound periodical titles (bound periodicals may be obtained through the Main; Science, Technology, and Business; or Microform Reading Rooms), and collects an array of American and foreign government publications.

right
Superman, number 32. New York: Superman, Inc. Jan.–Feb. 1945. Comic Book Collection, Serial and Government Publications Division. (Used with permission D.C. Comics).

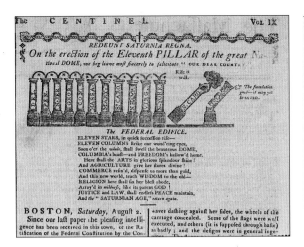

"The Federal Edifice," woodcut from The [Massachusetts] Centinel, *August 2, 1788. This rare eighteenth-century newspaper cartoon depicting the Federal Edifice shows New York becoming the eleventh state to ratify the U.S. Constitution. When thirteen pillars were in place, the structure would be complete and the Union cemented. Serial and Government Publications Division.*

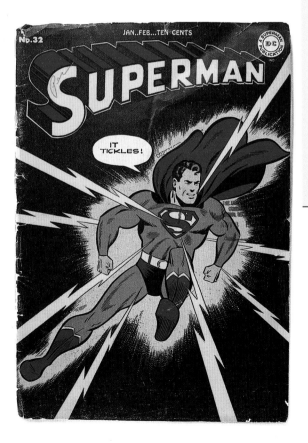

Thanks to the law requiring copyright deposit, the Serial and Government Publications Division has acquired approximately 100,000 comic books (6,000 titles), kept in special storage to prevent deterioration of the paper. The collection's oldest comic book is Popular Comics, *published in February 1936.*

The Federal Advisory Committee (FAC) Collection comprises materials deposited with the Library of Congress under the Federal Advisory Committee Act of 1972. The collection comprises 200,000 documents, including charters, annual reports, and background papers submitted to the Library of Congress by various committees, boards, commissions, councils, and other groups established to advise offices and agencies in the Executive Branch.

The Library's oldest original newspaper is Mercurius Publicas Comprising the Sum of Forraign Intelligence, *December 29, 1659.*

Prints and Photographs Division

The Library's interest in architecture and the fine arts began with Thomas Jefferson's collection of books on these subjects. The deposit of prints, photographs, posters, and architectural drawings, and other graphic materials required by the Copyright Act of 1870 formed the foundation of the Library's American holdings; an 1898 gift by Gertrude Hubbard added European master prints by artists such as Dürer and Rembrandt. In 1900, a separate Division of Prints was created; it was renamed the Prints and Photographs Division in 1944 to acknowledge the Library's acquisition of documentary and art photographs.

Accessed by researchers via the Prints and Photographs Division Reading Room (LM-337), the division's collections include more than 14 million images, ranging from original drawings by 200 artists of the "golden age" of American illustration (1870 through World War I), to photographic negatives of early American architecture, to editorial and political cartoons dating from before the American Revolution to the early twenty-first century. Treasures include sixteenth-century chiaroscuro woodcuts, and thousands of drawings by Civil War artist-correspondents, including Alfred Waud.

Daniel Hopfer (circa 1470–1536). "Trumpeters." Fine Prints Collection. Prints and Photographs Division.

Artist and illustrator James Montgomery Flagg (1877–1960) was his own model for this quintessential depiction of Uncle Sam in his World War I recruiting poster created in 1917. It is one of over 100,000 posters from all around the world in the Poster Collection. Prints and Photographs Division.

I WANT YOU
FOR U.S. ARMY
NEAREST RECRUITING STATION

An unidentified Union soldier of the U.S. Civil War. Ambrotype, circa 1863–65. The Library's holdings on the Civil War are particularly rich. Prints and Photographs Division.

left

Edward S. Curtis photographed this Flathead Indian chief near the turn of the twentieth century as part of his thirty-year mission, begun in 1896, to "form a comprehensive and permanent record of all the important tribes of the United States and Alaska that still retain to a considerable degree their primitive customs and traditions." Prints and Photographs Division.

right

Architect Cass Gilbert (1859–1934), whose work includes the Woolworth Building in New York City and the U.S. Supreme Court Building, created this watercolor rendering of the Dome of the Cathedral of Santa Maria del Fiore in Florence, Italy, at sunset. Architecture, Design and Engineering Collections, Prints and Photographs Division.

The *Prints and Photographs Division holds fine prints and drawings, cartoons, packaging labels, and posters; but photographic prints and negatives form 90 percent of its collection.*

The *Historic American Buildings Survey/Historic American Engineering Record (HABS/HAER), the Gottscho-Schleisner Collection of photographs, and collections of architectural drawings are among the materials that form one of the United States' most comprehensive architectural archives.*

The *Prints and Photographs Division holds the archives of two landmark documentary photography projects undertaken by the Farm Security Administration (FSA) and the Office of War Information (OWI) from 1935 to 1943. Thousands of images by photographers such as Dorothea Lange, Gordon Parks, and Jack Delano capture the experiences of Americans throughout the country during the Depression and World War II.*

Services to Congress
and Libraries

The *first copy of a Library of Congress catalog card was sold in 1901 for two cents and each additional copy, for one-half of one cent. In 1902, CDS's first full year of operation, 378,000 cards were sold. When card sales peaked in 1971, 74 million cards were purchased annually. Due to rapid technological changes, CDS catalog card sales declined to 360,000 in 1997—the final year of card distribution.*

The *first catalog card printed in the Library of Congress in 1898 was for* Money in Squabs, *a book by J. C. Long and G. H. Brinton. The last printed catalog card, sold by CDS in 1997, provided information on the 1990 book* War in the Pacific *by Clark G. Reynolds.*

Services to Congress and Libraries

previous page
*The dome of the Thomas
Jefferson Building behind a
U.S. flag. Photograph by
Rob Sokol.*

left
*Cataloging has come a long
way since the days of manual
cataloging shown in this World
War I era photograph—and
that is a good thing, for the
volume of books and other
materials to be cataloged has
continued to grow at an almost
overwhelming rate. Prints and
Photographs Division.*

following page
*The House of Representatives,
1866. Lithograph by Sachse.
Prints and Photographs
Division.*

The Library of Congress not only serves the public and members of Congress but, since the tenure of Librarian Herbert Putnam in the early twentieth century, other libraries. The Library of Congress has often been a resource in times of emergency, participating in international efforts to assist libraries and archives devastated by fire, flood, and war. The Library's efforts have included aid to the Academy of Sciences in St. Petersburg, Russia; conservation assistance in Florence, Italy; and donations of microfilm copies of Kuwaiti publications to Kuwait after the Persian Gulf War.

Cataloging Distribution Service

The Cataloging Distribution Service (CDS) serves the information needs of the Library of Congress and its worldwide constituencies by developing and marketing products and services that provide access to Library of Congress resources.

When a reader finds a book in any library in the world, the Library of Congress could well be guiding the search. Since 1901, the Card Division—which later became CDS—has made the Library of Congress classification, subject, and cataloging systems available for modest prices to libraries and information providers worldwide, thus helping to keep information retrieval practices consistent from library to library.

Throughout the years, CDS has adapted to changes in technology, providing cataloging records in computer format as early as 1968. These Machine Readable Cataloging (MARC-formatted) records became the standard for libraries and allowed them to use the MARC format either to create catalog records or to add the Library's cataloging records to their local files. More recently, CDS began publishing and distributing the Library's cataloging data and cataloging-related publications in multiple formats: web-based services, FTP delivery options, PDF print products, and traditional printed publications. CDS packages more than 300 cataloging and metadata resources in *Cataloger's Desktop* and the entire Library

PUBLISHED BY CASIMIR BOHN, WASHINGTON, D.C.

THE HOUSE OF REPRES

WASH

TATIVES, U.S. CAPITOL

TON, D.C.

of Congress Classification and complete subject headings in *Classification Web*, two web-based subscription services.

CDS also publishes standard subject authority information in machine-readable form and in the six-volume "red book," *Library of Congress Subject Headings* (LCSH). First published as one volume in 1909, as of 2010 LCSH contained more than 310,000 up-to-date headings and references, including "social networks." Other CDS publications in all formats include cataloging rules and application manuals, training manuals, and forty-one classification schedules from A to Z.

Congressional Research Service

If Congress has a question, the Congressional Research Service (CRS) provides the answer quickly, authoritatively, confidentially, and objectively. A descendent of the first "reference service" located in the Capitol when the early Library of Congress shared quarters with the nation's legislature, CRS (until 1970 called the Legislative Reference Service) was established by an act of Congress in 1914.

CRS anticipates and responds to Congress's needs for policy analysis and research in all areas of legislative and oversight interest. Throughout all stages of the legislative process, CRS experts work as shared staff to the Congress. Experts help all committees and Members of Congress identify and clarify policy problems and explore policy options, assess the implications of proposed policy alternatives, and monitor and assess program implementation and oversight. CRS helps inform Congress about legislative procedures and processes and provides timely responses to meet both immediate and long-term needs. The breadth and depth of its expertise enables CRS to move quickly to provide integrated, thorough analyses of complex issues.

Federal Library and Information Center Committee

The Federal Library and Information Center Committee (FLICC) was created in 1965 as the Federal Library Committee by joint action of the Library of Congress and the Bureau of the Budget (now the Office of Management and Budget). Comprising the directors of the four national libraries (the Library of Congress, the National Library of Medicine, the National Library of Education, and the National Agricultural Library), representatives of cabinet-level executive departments, and legislative, judicial, and independent federal agencies with major library programs, FLICC is headquartered at the Library of Congress and chaired by the Librarian of Congress.

FLICC serves as a forum for discussion of federal library and information policies, programs, and procedures. Its mission is to

From 1980 to 2010, the Library, in partnership with the National Endowment for the Humanities, spearheaded an effort to locate, catalog, and preserve newspapers published throughout the United States. More than 140,000 different newspaper titles were identified and cataloged and 75 million pages saved during the life of the program.

For forty years, the Library's Preservation Directorate has used events ranging from the National Book Festival to "Preservation Week," an American Library Association outreach and education initiative, to share with the public techniques of handling, conserving, and storing books, photographs, CDs, and family documents.

foster excellence in federal library and information services through interagency cooperation and to provide the most cost-effective and efficient information services possible to parent agency staffs, other government agencies, and the nation at large. By guiding and directing its FEDLINK (Federal Library and Information Network) program, FLICC aims to achieve better use of federal library and information center resources and facilities through professional development, promotion of services, and resource coordination.

Preservation and Conservation

From the moment anything enters the Library's collections, it receives the care required to preserve it. Printed items such as pamphlets and monographs are bound, newspapers microfilmed, motion pictures stored in refrigerated vaults, and manuscripts placed in temperature- and humidity-controlled storage. Acid is the worst enemy for papers manufactured since 1850; it makes paper weak and brittle, and pages eventually crack and flake away. The Library is a leader in developing and evaluating mass deacidification processes. Within the Preservation Directorate, the Preservation Research and Testing Division researches paper permanence; longevity of photographic, magnetic, CD-ROM, and other contemporary media; adhesives behavior; storage conditions; and other problems affecting the Library's diverse collections—and other collections around the world.

Mary Wooten in the Library's Conservation Office treating the autograph manuscript of Arnold Schoenberg's Pierrot Lunaire. *Photograph by Jim Higgins.*

The Conservation Division, renowned for its innovation, works on chemical stabilization and repair of maps, manuscripts, prints and drawings, books, and photographs. This work requires delicate skills and knowledge of chemistry. Creating the right storage environment is paramount. The Library's treasures are kept in cold-temperature vaults with controlled humidity, protected by a complex security system and an ozone-friendly, non-aqueous fire suppression system. Four of the rarest treasures—Jefferson's Rough Draft of the Declaration of Independence, Lincoln's first and second drafts of the Gettysburg Address, and George Mason's Virginia Declaration of Rights—are preserved in inert gas within custom-made containers, designed to virtually eliminate chemical interactions.

Public Progr
and Services

A Book is the

Best of Friends

STORMY

Public Programs and Services

An international resource for scholars and researchers, the Library also provides special programs and services to the public.

Ask a Librarian

Each year, thousands of people around the world click the "Ask a Librarian" link on the Library of Congress website and e-mail questions to Library staff. In each of the Library's reading rooms and divisions, including the Veterans History Project and the National Library Service for the Blind and Physically Handicapped, staff members are assigned to respond to these queries within five days, although most are answered within twenty-four hours. Through the Ask a Librarian chat feature, staff also spend several hours each week live online answering questions from the public. Ask a Librarian, developed by the worldwide library cooperative Online Computer Library Center (OCLC), is now used by several thousand libraries in the United States and overseas.

The Center for the Book

Established in 1977 by Public Law 95-129, the Center for the Book was created to "stimulate public interest and research in the role of the book in the diffusion of knowledge," and to encourage a nationwide interest in promoting and studying books, reading, and libraries. The Center's projects, symposia, lectures, book talks, exhibitions, and publications are funded primarily by private, tax-deductible contributions from individuals, corporations, and foundations or by funds from other government agencies.

Within the Library the Center is a focal point for celebrating the legacy of the printed word. The Center also works closely with other organizations, in the United States and abroad, to foster understanding of the vital role of literacy in society. Since 1984, the Center's efforts "to keep the book flourishing" have been helped by the creation of affiliated state-run centers in all fifty states, the District of Columbia, and the Virgin Islands and by partnerships

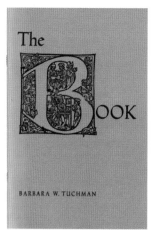

The

ᴮ OOK

BARBARA W. TUCHMAN

Cover of The Book, *a lecture presented at the Library of Congress in 1979 by historian and author Barbara W. Tuchman, an early member of the Center for the Book's advisory board. It is the first publication in the center's Viewpoint series.*

with eighty national and civic organizations. The Center for the Book has also been an inspiration and a model for similar initiatives in Great Britain, Canada, Russia, and South Africa.

Among the Center's noteworthy efforts are the National Book Festival, which draws more than 120,000 book lovers to the National Mall each year to celebrate reading and literacy, to hear authors read, and to have them sign their works (see page 125 for more information). The Center's Books & Beyond author series brings writers from all genres and from across the country and around the globe to the Library to talk about their work. These talks are made available as Library of Congress webcasts. The Center has also helped to publish more than 100 books and pamphlets about topics related to reading and libraries.

With a strong focus on reading and literacy among children and teens, the Center for the Book has developed extensive programming for young people. It oversees the Read.gov website, which features reading and literacy pages specifically designed for children, teens, adults, educators, and parents. It also partners with non-profits and corporate sponsors to conduct River of Words, an environmental art and poetry contest for young people, and Letters About Literature, an essay contest for students in grades 4 through 12.

In 2008 the Librarian of Congress appointed the first National Ambassador for Young People's Literature. During each two-year term, the ambassador travels the country raising awareness of the importance of young people's literature as it relates to lifelong literacy, education, and the development and betterment of young peoples' lives. The program is administered in collaboration with the Children's Book Council.

The Center's first symposium, sponsored with the U.S. Office of Education, also produced its first book: Television, the Book, and the Classroom *(1978). Since then, the Center has sponsored publication of forty-seven books, forty-one pamphlets, several research studies, and over a dozen posters.*

The Center for the Book pioneered using television to promote reading. Its first projects were "Read More About It!" lists on CBS Television (1979–98) and, on ABC Children's Television (1984–95), "Cap'n O. G. Readmore," an animated cat who knows a lot because he reads a lot.

Children's Literature Center

"To serve those who serve children" has been the mission of the Children's Literature Center since an act of Congress mandated its creation in 1963. The Center provides information and assistance to librarians, educators, publishers, writers, illustrators, scholars, and the public on the wealth of juvenile materials—some 500,000 children's books, periodicals, recordings, maps, and illustrations—housed in the Library of Congress. These items are found throughout the general and special collections and constitute a children's book collection that is so comprehensive that it is often a last, and sometimes unique resource. For example, first editions of *Little Women*, *The Adventures of Tom Sawyer*, and *The Wonderful Wizard of Oz* are housed in the Rare Book and Special Collections Division; maps for children in the Geography and Map Division; and television programs in the Motion Picture, Broadcasting, and Recorded Sound Division. Thus the Children's Literature Center serves as a

"The Platypus" and "The Sloth," two illustrations by Oliver Herford for A Child's Primer of Natural History, *Scribner's, 1899. Cabinet of American Illustration, Prints and Photographs Division.*

starting point for access to the Library's holdings, for searches of children's literature, and for research assistance.

The Center formulates the Library's selection policy for children's books and recommends and acquires—through appropriated and gift funds—materials from foreign language bibliographies, dealers' catalogues, and antiquarian book fairs. Its reading room (LJ-129) houses a reference collection for researchers.

"The Fire Bird," illustration by Edmund Dulac from Edmund Dulac's Fairy Book: Fairy Tales of the Allied Nations. *London, NY: Hodder & Stoughton, 1916. Children's Literature Center.*

During the U.S. occupation of Japan after World War II, Japanese publishers were required to deposit copies of their work at General Douglas MacArthur's headquarters. The Library acquired 1,500 Japanese children's books through this deposit.

The Library holds some 18,000 rare children's books, 100 of which are extremely rare. These include The Children's New Play-Thing *and* The Children's Bible, *both published in Philadelphia in 1763.*

Concerts, Broadcasts, and Film Showings

Thanks to the generosity and vision of two philanthropists—Elizabeth Sprague Coolidge and Gertrude Clarke Whittall—and several other benefactors, the Library of Congress has hosted thousands of concerts since the Coolidge Auditorium, an acoustic marvel, opened in 1925. In addition to performances funded by the Coolidge Foundation, the Library hosts concerts supported by the Whittall Foundation that showcase the five Stradivari instruments donated by Mrs. Whittall in the mid-1930s. In 1940, the Budapest String Quartet, after fleeing Nazi Germany, became the first artists-in-residence to perform regularly with these instruments. Since 1962, the quartet-in-residence has been the Juilliard String Quartet, and the Beaux Arts Trio has been trio-in-residence since 1982. In 1992, the Library's Music Division inaugurated a jazz series, and concerts celebrating the division's special collections have featured music by the Gershwins, Jerome Kern, Richard Rogers, and other figures of American musical theater.

In 2007, the Library established the Gershwin Prize for Popular Song to honor songwriters, interpreters, or singer/songwriters whose careers reflect lifetimes of achievement in promoting the genre of song as a vehicle for artistic expression and cultural understanding. In recent years, the prizewinner has participated in a concert at the Coolidge Auditorium followed by a special performance at the White House.

Many of the music foundations at the Library support the commissioning and performance of new works, and the Library has seen some historic musical premieres. Martha Graham, Aaron Copland, Artur Rubenstein, Nadia Boulanger, George Szell, Leonard Bernstein, Leopold Stokowski, Leontyne Price, and Samuel Barber are among the legendary artists who have appeared.

The Library also created the oldest chamber music broadcast series in the United States, now aired as *Concerts from the Library of Congress.* Starting with trial broadcasts from New York's NBC studios in 1930, the series evolved into live broadcasts from the Coolidge Auditorium in 1933. By the 1940s, broadcasts could be heard not only in the United States but also in Canada and Latin America. Now, millions around the world and more than a million nationwide tune in for Library of Congress broadcasts.

With the opening of the Mary Pickford Theater (Madison Building, Third Floor) in 1983, the Library began screening classic films from its diverse collection, including silent movies. Although

Martha Graham and Erick
Hawkins in the premiere of Aaron
Copland's Appalachian Spring *at*
the Library of Congress, October 30,
1944. Music Division.

Over the years, legendary jazz, blues, and folk artists, including Jelly Roll Morton, Leadbelly, Mississippi John Hurt, and Odetta, have performed or recorded in the Coolidge Auditorium.

The first national broadcast from the Coolidge Auditorium (1933) featured the first American appearance of the Adolf Busch String Quartet performing works by Beethoven, Busch, and Pizetti.

The Library holds an irreplaceable collection of dye-transfer Technicolor prints on safety stock, made between 1950 and 1954. These are the only color films not subject to fading, and the finest works have been shown in the Pickford Theater and at the Packard Campus.

the Pickford Theater is still used on rare occasions, in 2008 the Library moved its film program to the Packard Campus for Audio-Visual Conservation in Culpeper, Virginia (see page 95 for information about the Packard Campus). Programs include movies from the National Film Registry, a list of American films selected by the Librarian of Congress from nominations by the public and members of the National Film Preservation Board. The Board comprises representatives from the major movie industry guilds, producers, film critics, educators, and archivists, and its members advise the Librarian on films that are culturally, historically, and aesthetically important. Since 1989 the Librarian has added up to twenty-five films each year to the National Film Registry, including *Casablanca, Chinatown, City Lights, Dr. Strangelove, The Bride of Frankenstein, Blade Runner,* and *Steamboat Willy* (the first Disney cartoon featuring Mickey Mouse).

Duplication Services

The Duplication Services of the Library of Congress (LA-128) is a fee-for-service program responsible for copying items from the Library's collections. Established in 1938, with funds from the Rockefeller Foundation earmarked for "competently supplying distant investigators with microfilm and other photoduplicates of materials otherwise not available for use outside of Washington," Duplication Services has expanded its scope as demand and the number of photoreproductive formats have risen. It provides access to virtually all collections of the Library through photocopying, photographic, and digital services. Restrictions on duplication are based on the physical condition of the materials, copyright limitations, and legal restrictions on particular collections.

Duplication services are available on site and online to scholars, researchers, publishers, libraries, institutions, and members of the public. Fee schedules and order forms can be accessed on the Duplication Services website (http://www.loc.gov/duplicationservices). All orders must contain the Library Reproduction or Call Number, which can be obtained from Library online catalogs. Order forms must be faxed or mailed to Duplication Services.

Educational Outreach

The Library of Congress's Educational Outreach staff have developed two free programs to instruct teachers on how to use digitized materials to enhance students' learning skills. The programs, "Classroom Resources" and "Teaching with Primary Sources (TPS)," a professional development program for educators, use the Library's digitized primary source materials in an effort to spark students' critical thinking and deepen their content knowledge. The programs are based on teaching standards and focus on areas where the Library's collections are particularly strong: the U.S. Civil War, immigration, Native Americans, the Great Depression, and general topics about civics and government. Classroom resources include lesson plans, primary source sets, interactive online student activities, and higher-level questions about specific collections.

There are several ways in which teachers can participate in the TPS professional development program: 1) through on-site workshops at the Library, 2) online, and 3) through community partners, including universities and educational foundations. The curriculum can be customized, allowing districts and schools to create their own modules. To make TPS a truly national program, Educational Outreach staff are working to create partnerships in every state.

Interpretive Programs

From the rough draft of the Declaration of Independence, to Martin Waldseemüller's 1507 map marking the first time the name "America" appears on a landmass, to the searing political wit of cartoonist Herbert Block, to hundreds of Civil War portraits of enlisted soldiers, the Library of Congress Interpretive Programs Office (IPO) draws on the Library's unparalleled collections to mount thematic exhibitions that inform and inspire visitors. IPO develops and maintains ongoing exhibitions in the Thomas Jefferson Building, including *Exploring the Early Americas*, which examines indigenous cultures, the drama of the encounters between Native American

Interactive technology allows visitors to explore the art and architecture of the Thomas Jefferson Building's elaborate interiors that have inspired and captivated visitors since the building opened in 1897.

One permanent exhibition, Thomas Jefferson's Library, *literally surrounds visitors with a re-created version of Jefferson's library, 6,487 volumes that re-founded the Library of Congress after the British burned the U.S. Capitol in 1814. Through this close encounter, visitors learn how one of America's greatest thinkers was inspired through the world of books.*

With Malice Toward None: The Abraham Lincoln Bicentennial Exhibition *is among the major Library exhibitions that have traveled to other cultural institutions. The Library also loans materials from its collections to museums, historical societies, and libraries around the world.*

One ongoing Library of Congress exhibition is "Exploring the Early Americas," which features selections from the Jay Kislak Collection and highlights the pivotal changes caused by the meeting of American and European cultures.

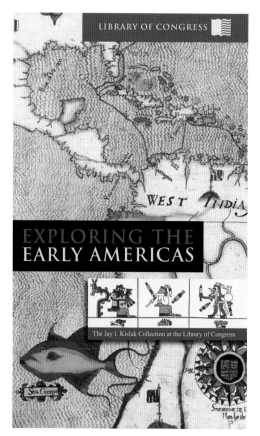

cultures and Europeans, and the resulting changes caused by the meeting of two worlds. The Graphic Arts Galleries offer a broad sampling of the Library's rich visual art collections; the George and Ira Gershwin Room features a display of memorabilia and music associated with one of America's greatest composer-lyricist teams; and the Bob Hope Gallery of American Entertainment invites visitors to explore the interplay of politics and entertainment by presenting materials related to Hope and other entertainers who reflected and influenced the political climate of their times.

IPO develops and mounts temporary exhibitions that share new acquisitions, showcase long-held collections, or mark anniversaries, such as the 500th anniversary of the first sustained contacts between Native American people and Europeans (1992) and the sesquicentennial of the American Civil War (2011–15). IPO also organizes auxiliary programming such as online exhibitions (http://www.loc.gov/exhibits/all), symposia, exhibit tours, and teacher-training workshops that support and use the exhibition program.

National Book Festival

The National Book Festival was cofounded in 2001 by First Lady Laura Bush and organized by the Library of Congress's Center for the Book to celebrate reading, literacy, and creativity. Held annually on the National Mall in Washington, D.C., the festival attracts more than 120,000 visitors each year who hear talks and readings by some of America's best known authors and poets, purchase books, attend book signings, and learn about literacy efforts in their states. The event features dozens of authors in specialized pavilions: Children, Fiction & Fantasy, History & Biography, Mysteries & Thrillers, Teens & Children and Poetry & Prose. Sue Grafton, John Grisham, John Irving, David McCullough, Walter Mosley, Joyce Carol Oates, George Pelecanos, Paul Theroux, and Tom Wolfe are among the well-known novelists, suspense writers, historians, journalists, biographers, and poets who have participated in the festival. Events geared toward children and teens include readings and storytelling by children's authors such as Judy Blume, performances by Sesame Street characters, and entertaining and educational activities that promote reading.

So that book-lovers around the country can participate in the event, the Library posts webcasts of the festival on its website. Podcasts of interviews with authors participating in the festival are available free of charge through the Library's website or on iTunes.

National Library Service for the Blind and Physically Handicapped

Now the Library's second largest service division (after the Congressional Research Service), the National Library Service for the Blind and Physically Handicapped (NLS) began as a talking-book program established by Congress in 1931 to serve blind adults. The program, then called the Division for the Blind, expanded in 1952 to include children, and in 1962, Congress added musical materials, including scores, textbooks, and books about music in Braille and large print, and elementary instruction for voice and various musical instruments.

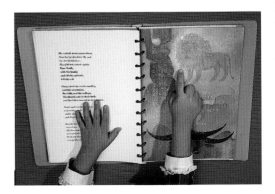

Girl reading Noah's Ark *in Braille, National Library Service for the Blind and Physically Handicapped.*

In 1966, the program expanded to become the Division for the Blind and Physically Handicapped, serving individuals with physical impairments that prevent the reading of standard print. At the same time, the offices were moved from crowded quarters in the Jefferson and Adams Buildings to rental facilities on Taylor Street, in northwest Washington, where they remain.

With an annual budget exceeding $70 million, NLS now serves, free of charge, any resident of the United States or any American citizen living abroad who is unable to use standard print materials as a result of a visual or physical limitation. Materials selected for NLS circulation include in-demand items like bestsellers, biographies, fiction, and how-to books, as well as titles in Spanish and current magazines. Registered borrowers learn of new books added to the collection through bimonthly publications. Available books are accessible to every institution in a cooperating network of fifty-six regional and sixty-five subregional libraries via the International Union Catalog on the Internet. Playback equipment is also loaned free to readers for as long as recorded materials provided by NLS and its cooperating libraries are borrowed.

An additional appropriation to the U.S. Postal Service allows books and materials to be mailed as Free Matter for the Blind or Handicapped. Under a special provision of U.S. copyright law and with permission of authors and publishers of works not covered by the provision, NLS selects and produces full-length books and magazines in Braille and on cassette and digital cartridges.

The program is now transitioning to state-of-the-art digital talking books, audiobooks, and Web-Braille. As digital playback machines and media are phased in at libraries nationwide, analog cassettes and equipment are phased out. Web-Braille, a web-based service, is increasingly available to provide access to thousands of Braille books, magazines, and music scores. To read these files, patrons or participating network libraries must use special equipment such as a Braille display or Braille embosser. In addition, through the online Braille and Audio Reading Download (BARD) service, patrons who register to use BARD can download audio book files.

Office of Communications

The Office of Communications coordinates all external communications with the Library's various offices and divisions and works directly with the news media and online communities to share news about the Library's programs, operations and events. The office is the content manager for many of the Library's social media projects, manages all on-site film and video productions involving outside parties, and is the primary office responsible for disseminating all staff and emergency communications. It publishes a monthly magazine, a calendar of events, a weekly staff newsletter, brochures, and various web features and maintains an official photo archive regarding Library events and other related matters.

Office of Scholarly Programs
Created in 1990, the Office of Scholarly Programs (LJ-120) facilitates the exchange of information and ideas throughout the worldwide community of scholars using the resources of the Library of Congress. The Office draws scholars to the Library for extended periods of research, runs a number of competitions including the Henry A. Kissinger Award, and awards fellowships to top scholars. Through a major partnership with the British Research Councils, the Office brings approximately two dozen students from British universities who are working on their dissertations to the Library for

Charles Locke, "The Library." Lithograph, 192?. Fine Prints Collection, Prints and Photographs Division.

three to six months. For the Summer Research Institutes program, university faculty bring junior scholars to the Library for a course of lectures, discussions, and in-depth research in the collections.

The Office also organizes formal colloquia, lectures, and symposia to present the fruits of scholars' research to the Library. By encouraging the pursuit and sharing of information among the wider scholarly community and Library staff, the office cuts across national, disciplinary, and institutional boundaries to expand the frontiers of knowledge.

The Head of the Office of Scholarly Programs directs the John W. Kluge Center and the Poetry and Literature Center.

The John W. Kluge Center

When Metromedia President John W. Kluge wanted to create an academic center at the Library of Congress in October 2000 to bring Congress together with the best of the world's scholars, he donated $60 million to the Library to realize his dream. It was the largest single monetary donation in the Library's 200-year history. Today the Kluge Center, based in the Jefferson Building, brings together some of the best minds in the scholarly world to spend six to eleven months accessing the Library's unparalleled resources and interacting with policymakers in Washington, D.C. The Center also brings the most promising new career Fellows to the Library to use the collections for research. The Kluge Center sponsors symposia, lectures, book talks, and conferences, as well as a series of talks by scholars on their particular areas of research. Approximately every two years, the Center awards a $1,000,000 Kluge prize recognizing lifetime achievement in the humanities, which is sometimes split between two scholars. Past winners of the Kluge Prize have included Jaroslav Pelikan, credited with single-handedly bringing the Eastern or Orthodox tradition into the hitherto largely Western story of Christian tradition, and John Hope Franklin, an eminent historian of the African-American experience in the United States. Another prizewinner, Yu Ying-shih, Emeritus Professor of East Asian Studies and History at Princeton University, is described by his peers as "the greatest Chinese intellectual historian of our generation," while prizewinner Romila Thapar is one of the world's foremost experts on the history of early India.

Other resident scholars who have delivered lectures at the Library include sociologist Neil Smelser, whose 2006 talk focused on the power of terrorist ideologies, and anthropologist Emiko Ohnuki-Tierney, the Kluge Center's Chair of Modern Culture, 2009, who spoke about the symbolism of cherry blossoms in Japanese culture and history. Former President of the Czech

Republic and Kluge Chair in Modern Culture, 2005, Vaclev Havel gave a May 2005 lecture urging support for dissidents opposing dictatorial regimes around the world.

Poetry and Literature Center
Since 1936, when Archer M. Huntington endowed "the Chair of Poetry of the English Language," poetry has been a visible and dynamic force at the Library. During Archibald MacLeish's tenure as Librarian from 1939 to 1944, the Consultant in Poetry became an annual appointment. Joseph Auslander was the first to fill the post, followed by a virtual Who's Who of American literature, including Robert Penn Warren, Robert Lowell, Elizabeth Bishop, Robert Frost, and Gwendolyn Brooks. In 1986, the consultancy was given additional status by the U.S. Congress, which changed the position to Poet Laureate, Consultant in Poetry. Howard Nemerov, Rita Dove, Robert Hass, Robert Pinsky, Billy Collins, and W. S. Merwin are among the Poets Laureate who have served since then.

Poetry Consultant Maxine Kumin in the Poetry Room of the Library of Congress with a fourth-grade class from a Washington elementary school, December 11, 1981. Publishing Office.

right
Poet Laureate W. S. Merwin. Photograph by Matt Valentine.

far right
Poet Laureate Kay Ryan. Photograph by Christina Koci Hernandez.

The Poet Laureate not only organizes readings at the Library, but also promotes poetry through readings and presentations throughout the country. He or she has offices in the Poetry and Literature Center (LJ-A02), which administers the oldest reading series in the Washington, D.C. area, and one of the oldest in the United States. The series began in the 1940s, and since 1951 has received strong support from endowments from the Gertrude Clarke Whittall Foundation. It features fiction as well as poetry readings, lectures, symposia, and occasional dramatic performances.

The Center also awards prizes for poetry. The biennial, privately funded Bobbitt National Prize for Poetry is given for the most distinguished book of poetry published by an American in the preceding two years. The Witter Byner Foundation provides funds for a fellowship to encourage poets and poetry, and the winners are selected by the Poet Laureate and the Library.

The Center also sponsors evening readings and the popular "Poetry at Noon" series, which are open to the public.

Publishing

For more than 200 years, the Library of Congress has produced an increasing stream of pamphlets, monographs, books, and other materials that open its ever-growing collections and activities to the nation and the world. Today, the Library's publishing activities can be divided into the categories of *specialized* and *general* publications.

Specialized publications are defined by the needs of individual

Robert Frost and Carl Sandburg at the Library of Congress, 1960. Publishing Office.

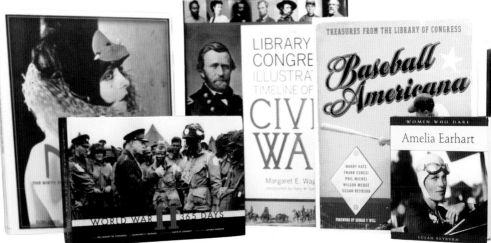

In 2010, W. W. Norton, in association with the Library of Congress, produced the first anthology to gather poems by the forty-three Poets Laureate of the United States.

below
An array of books produced by the Library of Congress Publishing Office.

constituencies served, for example, by the Congressional Research Service, the Copyright Office, the National Library Service for the Blind and Physically Handicapped, the Cataloging Distribution Service, the Federal Library and Information Center Committee, and the Federal Research Division.

Much broader audiences are served by the Library of Congress Publishing Office (LCPO), which is the center of the Library's General Publishing Program. LCPO has the broad mission of sharing the Library's collections and activities—as well as the knowledge of the Library's subject-area specialists—with scholars, researchers, the legal community, and the general public. To fulfill this mandate, LCPO produces a wide variety of materials, releasing more than twenty new publications each year. These include:

- Institutional publications and series, including resource guides to Library holdings and collections, as well as works on the Library's history, art, and architecture;
- Scholarly works and "trade" books (books published for a general audience and distributed through booksellers), including books to accompany Library of Congress exhibitions;
- Consumer products such as calendars, postcard books, notecards, and posters based on items from the Library's collections.

LCPO's writers, editors, and researchers work in collaboration with curators, reference librarians, subject specialists, and others throughout the Library, as well as specialists from outside the Library, in creating accurate, authoritative works. To produce the

resulting publications, LCPO routinely engages in mutually benefi-
cial co-publishing and other partnership arrangements with trade
and university publishers. To date, LCPO, with its private sector
partners, has published celebrated works on topics ranging from
baseball, silent film, and women's history to World War II, African
American history, and the artistry of major American photographers. Recent major releases include a lively, groundbreaking
examination of maps as cultural documents; an anthology of works
by America's Poets Laureate, Consultants in Poetry (who reside,
during their tenures, in the Library of Congress, see page 129); and
a lavishly illustrated, narrative timeline of the American Civil War.

The United States Copyright Office

The vital relationship between the Copyright Office (LM-401)
and the Library of Congress was built upon the bedrock of the
Constitution (Article 1, Section 8), which gives Congress the power
to enact laws establishing a system of copyright in the United States.
"Copyright" means, literally, the right to copy.

Congress enacted the first copyright law in May 1790, and clerks
of U.S. District Courts recorded the first claims. However, no coher-
ent system for tracking or maintaining the deposits submitted with
claims existed. Upon the urging of Librarian of Congress Ainsworth
Rand Spofford, in 1870 Congress passed a law that centralized the
copyright system in the Library and required all authors to deposit
in the Library two copies of every book, pamphlet, map, print, and
piece of music registered in the United States. The Copyright Office
became a separate department of the Library of Congress in 1897,
coinciding with the move to a new building.

Copyright protection now covers original works of authorship,
which include literary, dramatic, musical, architectural, cartographic, choreographic, pantomimic, pictorial, graphic, and sculptural
works, sound recordings, and motion pictures and other audiovisu-
al creations. The archives maintained by the Copyright Office are an
important record of America's cultural and historical heritage.
Containing nearly 45 million individual cards, the Copyright Card
Catalog housed in the Madison Building is the world's largest card
catalog and comprises an index to copyright registrations in the

---

*The Copyright Office annually processes and registers 600,000
claims.*

*The Copyright Office has handled more than 34 million copy-
right registrations and transfers since 1790.*

United States from 1870 through 1977. Post-1977 registrations are available online on the Copyright Office's website. Much of the literary, musical, artistic, and scientific production of the United States and of many foreign countries is recorded here, providing an important supplement to the main catalog of the Library of Congress as a research tool.

Deposits received through the copyright system provide hundreds of thousands of items yearly for the Library's collections. In 2008 it released the electronic Copyright Office (eCO) system, which allows online copyright registration and offers users faster processing times, online status tracking, secure online payment, and lower filing fees.

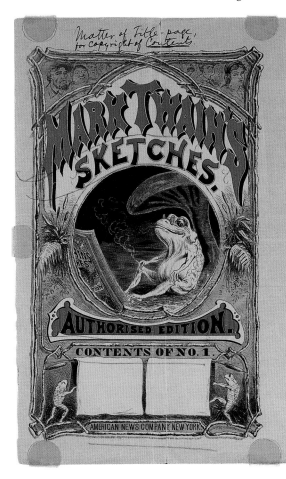

In 1874, Samuel Clemens wrote to Librarian of Congress Ainsworth Rand Spofford requesting copyright for a new pamphlet by "Mark Twain." Rare Book and Special Collections Division.

More recently, the Copyright Office worked with internal Library service units and external organizations to build a robust electronic copyright deposit system. As part of its Digital Collection Management Initiative, the Library is now able to collect electronic scholarly journals that are available only in digital format. The electronic deposit system permits copyright owners of these journals to deposit their publications into a digital archive maintained by the Library.

Visitor Programming and Services

The Library of Congress, the Nation's Library, is open to all. Everyone is welcome to view its historic buildings and exhibitions, and everyone over age sixteen may use its collections. While researchers generally work in any of the twenty-one reading rooms, most visitors typically focus on the historic Jefferson Building with its architectural and artistic beauty and its engaging exhibitions. Information about visiting and using the Library is available at the public entrances in the Jefferson and Madison Buildings.

The Visitor Services Office offers daily guided tours of the Jefferson Building and the exhibitions. In addition, the Library's website (www.loc.gov) lists the schedule of themed tours, gallery talks, and other special public programs, as well as general information about visiting the Library.

To accommodate visitors who wish to look around on their own, the Library has developed several self-guided tools. Stand-alone interactives are available to help visitors explore the beauty of the historic surroundings and the collections, as are color and large-print brochures that can also serve as guides and mementos. In 2008, the Library introduced the "Passport to Knowledge," which visitors can use with the interactive myLOC kiosks in the Jefferson Building. When they return home, they can use their passports to create their own web pages by bookmarking objects for further study at the Library's myLOC.gov website.

The Library's cafeteria, on the sixth floor of the Madison Building (LM-625), serves breakfast and lunch, and a coffee shop and snack bar on the ground floor of the Madison Building are also open to the public. The Library of Congress Shop, offering unique items based on the Library's collections, is located on the ground floor of the Jefferson Building near the First Street entrance.

Young Readers Center

For the first time in its history, the Library of Congress now has a space devoted to the reading interests of children and teens. Housed in the historic Thomas Jefferson Building (LJ-G29), the Young Readers Center offers young visitors (accompanied by an adult) an opportunity to read a current or classic book from an up-to-date collection of non-circulating titles, browse kid-friendly websites on the Center's computers, or attend programs especially designed for young readers. The Center's media room also lets visitors view webcasts of young adult and children's authors who have appeared at the National Book Festival. The Young Readers Center is a special space in the Library of Congress designed for adults and children to enjoy together.

A *train rushes through the night past dark mountains and deep woods. Hiding on the train, eleven-year-old twins on the run from the circus clutch a mysterious birthday card. So began* The Exquisite Corpse Adventure, *a serial story written for the Library of Congress's Read.gov website. Beginning in September 2009, a new installment of the story was released every two weeks throughout the following year, each chapter written and illustrated by a different celebrated writer and artist. Educational support materials were also provided on the website to help all readers—young people, families, teachers, and librarians—enjoy* The Exquisite Corpse Adventure *together.*

CREATING THE UNITED STATES

Preserving the Past,
Informing the Future:
The Library of Congress
in the Digital Age

54th Play not the Peacock, looking every where about you, to See if you be well Deck't, if your Shoes fit well if your Stokings Sit neatly, and Cloths handsomely.

55: Eat not in the Streets, nor in yͤ House, out of Season

56: Associate yourself with Men of good Quality if you Esteem your own Reputation; for 'tis better to be alone than in bad Company

57: In walking up and Down in a House, only with One in Company if he be Greater than yourself, at the first give him the Right hand and Stop not till he does and be not the first that turns, and when you do turn let it be with your face towards him, if he be a Man of Great Quality, walk not with him Cheek by Joul but Somewhat behind him; but yet in Such a Manner that he may easily Speak to you

58: Let your Conversation be without Malice or Envy, for 'tis a Sig of a Tractable and Commendable Nature: And in all Causes of Passion mit Reason to Govern

59th Never express any thing unbecoming, nor act agᵗ yͤ Rules Moral before your inferiours

60th Be not immodest in urging your Freinds to Discover a Secret

61st Utter not base and frivilous things amongst grave and Learn'd Men, nor very Difficult Questians or Subjects, among the Ignorant or things hard to be believed, Stuff not your Discourse with Sentences amongst your Betters nor Equals

62 Speak not of Doleful Things in a Time of Mirth or at the Table; Speak not of Melancholy Things as Death and Wounds, and if others Mention them Change if you can the Discourse tell not your Dreams, but to your intimate Friend

63 A Man ought not to value himself of his Atchievements, or rare Qualities Virtue or Kindred

Preserving the Past, Informing the Future: The Library of Congress in the Digital Age

"**W**e are witnessing the transformation to a society where instantly available, reliable, and credible information will be as indispensable as electricity, water and transportation, and we are proud to play a large role in this change," said Librarian of Congress James H. Billington in a 2007 statement to Congress. In fact, at that point the Library of Congress had already been preparing for more than a decade to face the technological challenges of the twenty-first century and meet the public's need for valid, trustworthy information.

Through a combination of foresight, experimentation, and public-private enterprise, the Library of Congress is now a leader among large institutions in making its collections available via the Internet. Its robust website, www.loc.gov, has pages devoted to its own collections, catalogs, and exhibitions; federal legislative activity in Congress; information from the U.S. Copyright Office; and sections developed specifically for researchers, teachers, visitors, publishers, and librarians. But making this information available online was only the first step toward meeting the digital challenge. The Library has also partnered with other government agencies and corporate entities to digitize rare and at-risk materials, expanded its online presence and developed new tools to help the public better access its collections, and used technology to connect with and inform the community about the vast resources available at the Library of Congress.

Creating Partnerships Around the World

The Library of Congress has taken a leadership role in joint projects with federal agencies, non-profit groups, and other libraries that share its goal of expanding access to rare and important historical and cultural materials. Through partnerships with the private sector the Library has access to financial resources and technology that would otherwise be outside its reach. For example, the Library is working with the Newspaper Association of America to develop a process to collect copyrights for digital-only materials and is reaching out to the publishing community for help. It has also contracted with Amazon.com to provide print-on-demand services for 50,000 rare or out-of-print books that have been digitized and are no longer under copyright. These and other initiatives require the Library to work closely with outside entities to develop standards and systems that can solve the problems and take advantage of the opportunities brought about by digitization.

The following are a few of the key programs and partnerships the Library of Congress has established to meet the digital challenge.

World Digital Library
In a June 2005 speech to the U.S. National Commission for the United Nations Educational Scientific and Cultural Organization (UNESCO), Librarian of Congress James H. Billington proposed establishing an Internet-only World Digital Library (WDL) to bring together significant primary materials from around the world. He said, "A World Digital Library would make these collections available free of charge to anyone accessing the Internet, and it could well have the salutary effect of bringing people together by celebrating the depth and uniqueness of different cultures in a single global undertaking." Working collaboratively with organizations, museums, and libraries in nations around the world, the Library launched the WDL website in April 2009 with content from or about all 192 countries belonging to UNESCO.

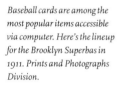

Baseball cards are among the most popular items accessible via computer. Here's the lineup for the Brooklyn Superbas in 1911. Prints and Photographs Division.

The WDL's principal objectives are to promote international and intercultural understanding; expand the volume and variety of cultural content on the Internet; provide resources for educators, scholars, and general audiences; and narrow the digital divide within and between countries. To address this last goal, grants from foundations and corporations have been targeted to help developing countries or regions digitize materials for the site.

*National Digital Information Infrastructure
and Preservation Program (NDIIPP)*

The Library's Office of Strategic Initiatives is leading the NDIIPP, a strategic initiative mandated by Congress in 2000 to collect and preserve at-risk digital content of cultural and historical importance. The NDIIPP has established a national network of partners, including federal agencies, state and local governments, academia, professional and non-profit organizations, and commercial entities. Network members are committed to selecting, collecting, preserving, and making accessible at-risk digital information including websites with limited life spans. By 2010, the NDIIPP had grown to more than 130 organizations seeking to preserve a wide range of records found only in digital format and working to establish standards for digital preservation.

The NDIIPP's efforts include collecting websites and blogs related to subjects of historic and cultural importance (e.g. the Iraq war, U.S. elections, Congress, and law-related blogs); helping state archives, libraries, historical societies, and other agencies safeguard vital digital information; and partnering with other libraries and federal entities to preserve public government websites at the end of the George W. Bush presidential administration. The NDIIPP is also working with external organizations on a system that allows copyright owners to electronically deposit their publications into a digital archive maintained by the Library; awarding grants to private sector partners to preserve creative works, including photographs, cartoons, motion pictures, sound recordings and video games, in digital formats; and participating in a joint effort by federal agencies to define common guidelines, methods and practices to use when digitizing historical content.

Digitizing Content for the Web
The Library of Congress is a member of an alliance of research libraries that works with the Internet Archive, a non-profit organization founded in 1996 to build an Internet library offering permanent access to historical collections in digital format. With a $2 million grant from the Alfred P. Sloan Foundation, the Library and the Internet Archive digitized 60,000 at-risk "brittle books" from the Library's special collections and made them available on the Internet Archive's website, www.archive.org. Together, the Library and the Internet Archive developed the open-source page-turner, which greatly enhances the usability of digital books, and they collect websites of historical and cultural importance, including 30,000 websites related to the 9/11 terrorist attacks. The Library will also have the Internet Archive scan 8,000 reels of microfilm of telephone directories for genealogical research.

To digitize and provide free public access to historic American newspapers in the public domain, the Library of Congress and the National Endowment for the Humanities participate in the National Digital Newspaper Program. Since March 2007, the Library has made newspapers accessible on the Chronicling America website, which contains a free searchable database of pages from historic American newspapers published between 1880 and 1922.

Online Photo Sharing
As part of a plan to broaden access to the Library's photo collections and explore new ways to acquire information about these collections, in 2008 the Library added several thousand photos without copyright restrictions to Flickr, an online photo sharing service. Flickr users can add descriptive terms to photos, providing Library curators with new data regarding those photos about which the Library has limited information. In less than one year, the Library's photos on Flickr drew more than 10 million views and generated thousands of comments and e-mails.

The Commons, a Flickr initiative introduced when the Library launched its project, allows photos with "no known copyright restriction" to be posted online. Consequently, dozens of other libraries, museums and archives around the world began sharing selections from their photo archives within the Commons framework.

Using Technology to Connect to the Community

For several decades, the Library of Congress has been committed to using technology to reach new audiences and share its peerless collections with the public. In the early 1990s, the American Memory pilot project reproduced selected Library collections and primary sources—the Gettysburg Address, U.S. Civil War photographs, notebooks in Walt Whitman's own hand, and others—on disc for schools and libraries. Three of the American Memory photograph collections were made available over the Internet in 1994. The National Digital Library Program, formed in October 1994 with support from the private sector, Congress, and the vice president of the United States, assembled a core of American historical and cultural primary source material in digital form. By 1999, the Library had 5 million American history items online or on CD-ROMs.

Panoramic maps are among the items researchers may find on the Library's American Memory web page. This map, sketched by C. J. Dyer, gives a bird's-eye-view of Phoenix, Arizona, as it was in 1885. Geography and Map Division.

More recently, the Library has initiated a number of programs and services to connect with people who may not be able to visit its buildings or access the collections. One service, Ask a Librarian, lets people around the world e-mail queries to Library staff (see page 115). An electronic Copyright Office (eCO) system provides for online copyright registration, offering users faster processing times, online status tracking, secure online payment, and lower filing fees (see also page 133). The Library's Educational Outreach staff offers resources and services based on the Library's online primary source materials to K–12 teachers and students. Staff members also manage the Teaching with Primary Sources program that instructs educators about how they can use digitized collections to enhance students' learning skills in the classroom (see page 123 for more information). For children, teens, parents and educators, the Read.gov website contains resources from the Library designed to encourage young people to read books and to interest them in learning about the authors and illustrators who create them. The National Library Service for the Blind and Physically Handicapped uses digital technologies, including Web-Braille, to provide patrons with audiobooks, state-of-the art digital talking books, and Braille books, magazines and music scores (see pages 125–126).

Increasingly the Library is adopting new technologies, and expanding the scope of its website to allow people around the world to virtually experience the Library of Congress.

Digital Communication Tools
Facebook. YouTube. Twitter. The Library of Congress participates in social networking sites to connect with people interested in Library events, photos, videos, and other aspects of its collections. The Library's blogs inform audiences about events at the Library, while subscribers to its RSS feeds and e-mail update service receive up-to-date announcements about areas of the Library that interest them, from general news and events to specific information on copyright legislation, digital preservation, or other topics. Through iTunes U, an area of Apple's iTunes Store that offers free educational audio and video files, users can download Library content. Each year, hundreds of events held at the Library—lectures, readings, interviews, conferences, and symposia—are captured and made accessible as webcasts or podcasts on www.loc.gov.

The Library of Congress Experience
The "Library of Congress Experience" uses innovative technology to integrate the look and feel of exhibitions in the Thomas Jefferson Building with content on the Library's website. Visitors to the

IGNORANCE IS THE CVRSE OF GOD
KNOWLEDGE THE WING
WHEREWITH WE FLY TO HEAVEN.

Thomas Reid's mural depicting Knowledge graces the second floor, north corridor, of the Thomas Jefferson Building. Photograph by Carol Highsmith.

Jefferson Building can obtain and use a "Passport to Knowledge" with interactive kiosks to explore architectural details of the building and closely examine some of its treasured collections. Each passport has a unique barcode that allows users to connect to personalized accounts on the Library's interactive companion site, myLOC.gov. As visitors physically and virtually navigate through the Library's collections, they can bookmark items of interest and create their own web page. Then, at home or school, they can access their customized collections to further explore the Library's vast resources online. The myLOC.gov site also provides educational resources to help teachers transform a visit to the Library into a meaningful learning experience for students.

In the coming years, the Library of Congress will continue to adopt and adapt to new technology to remain connected to the public, researchers, teachers, Congress, federal agencies, and private businesses—all of the people who want access to this wonderful resource, the Nation's Library.

Appendix I Using the Library of Congress

Researchers wishing to use Library collections in the public reading rooms or reference centers, and to request materials from the stacks, must have a free, Library-issued Reader Identification Card. Researchers can obtain these cards by presenting photo-identification showing a current address (e.g. a valid driver's license, passport, or state-issued identification card) at the Reader Registration Station, Room LM-140, in the Madison Building. After a researcher completes the computerized self-registration process, Library staff check the information, take an identification photo, have the researcher provide a digitized signature, and issue a printed plastic card. The Reader Identification Cards are issued to anyone sixteen years or older and are valid for two years.

The Library aims to make each research visit as efficient, useful, and rewarding as possible. While some basic research information is available at the Research Guidance desk in the Reader Registration Station, new researchers may want to begin their work

Visitors relax outside the Jefferson Building of the Library of Congress. Photograph by Abby Brack.

by visiting the Reference Assistance Room on the first floor of the Jefferson Building, adjacent to the Main Reading Room. Reference librarians are available to help researchers use the catalogs and reference materials, make referrals to other reading rooms or bibliographic sources, and help locate materials. In addition, the Library's Humanities and Social Sciences Division, also located in the Jefferson Building, offers a general orientation about using the Library's collections. Dates and times are posted on the Library's website.

The Library of Congress Online Catalog provides information about the collections to researchers both on and off site. Registered readers may create an individual account number to request materials from the Library's general collections via the online catalog for use in the Library's reading rooms. Additionally workstations in all reading rooms provide access to a wide variety of subscription databases, and free WiFi is available in public research areas.

Reserved facilities are available for those whose research requires extensive use of the Library. There are study shelves for users of the General Collections who wish to hold a limited number of books for an extended time. Application for a study shelf should be made to the Research Facilities Officer in the Main Reading Room.

Finding Aids and Other Divisional Research Guidance

Many reading rooms have specific catalogs and reference sources, both electronic and printed. There are finding aids, including indexes, bibliographies, and specialized card files, to help researchers locate items such as photographs, letters, music scores, or maps within a specialized collection. For example, the Manuscript Division Reading Room has guides to the contents of its largest individual collections; the Prints and Photographs Division Reading Room maintains browsable vertical files containing photographic prints or photocopied images from the most in-demand collections while also offering printed finding aids to various division collections; and the Rare Book and Special Collections Reading Room has card files describing individual collections. Each reading room has its own web page providing detailed information about its collections, services, and hours; some reading rooms also offer research orientation or tours specific to their collections or services.

While laptop computers are permitted in the reading rooms, most reading rooms restrict items that can be brought into the room. Lockers and/or cloakrooms are available. Most reading rooms also have self-service copiers operated by copy cards obtainable at vending machines throughout the Library or at the Duplication Services Walk-Up Counter (Adams Building, Room LA-128).

Although the Library of Congress was established in 1800, the office of Librarian was not created until 1802. The law creating the office stipulated that the Librarian of Congress was to be appointed by the president. In fact, Congress had no formal role in the appointment process until 1897, when the Senate gained the privilege of confirming the president's selection. The law did not prescribe any special qualifications or specify a term of office, although in the twentieth century the precedent was established that the Librarian is appointed for life. The Librarian of Congress had little formal authority until 1897, when by law the Librarian was given sole responsibility for making the institution's rules and regulations and appointing its staff. As of 2010, there have been thirteen Librarians:

John J. Beckley (1802–1807)

A political ally of President Thomas Jefferson and the first clerk of the House of Representatives, Beckley was appointed Librarian by Jefferson on January 29, 1802. His salary as Librarian could not exceed two dollars a day. Beckley died on April 8, 1807.

Patrick Magruder (1807–1815)

A local politician and former congressman, Magruder was appointed Librarian by President Jefferson on November 7, 1807—ten days after being named clerk of the House of Representatives. He served in the posts concurrently. On August 24, 1814, the British captured Washington and burned the U.S. Capitol, including the Library of Congress, which was in the Capitol's north wing. After a congressional investigation about the loss of the Library and the use of Library funds, in January 1815, Magruder resigned his position of clerk of the House and, by inference, the office of Librarian of Congress.

George Watterston (1815–1829)

Novelist and journalist Watterston was appointed Librarian by President James Madison on March 21, 1815. The capital's leading man of letters, Watterston was the Librarian who received Jefferson's library in 1815 and adopted Jefferson's basic classification scheme. A partisan Whig, he was replaced in 1829 by a Democrat appointed by newly elected President Andrew Jackson.

John Silva Meehan (1829–1861)

President Jackson appointed Meehan, a local printer, publisher, and a Democrat, Librarian on May 28, 1829. Meehan continued as Librarian until May 1861, when President Abraham Lincoln replaced him with one of his own political supporters.

John. G. Stephenson (1861–1864)
Appointed Librarian by President Lincoln on May 24, 1861, Stephenson was a physician from Terre Haute, Indiana. An ardent bookman and a Republican, Stephenson served as Librarian for only three years. He resigned on December 31, 1864.

Ainsworth Rand Spofford (1864–1897)
Assistant Librarian of Congress Spofford was elevated to the Librarian's office when President Lincoln appointed him on December 31, 1864. In 1896, on the eve of the Library's move into its first separate building, the leaders of the American Library Association (ALA) made it clear that they hoped the seventy-one-year-old Spofford would step aside in favor of a younger and more progressive professional librarian. One day after President William McKinley nominated John Russell Young to be the new Librarian, Young named Spofford as Chief Assistant Librarian, an important job that Spofford held until his death.

John Russell Young (1897–1899)
President McKinley appointed former journalist and diplomat Young Librarian on June 30, 1897. He was the first Librarian confirmed by the Senate, following the reorganization of the Library approved in February 1897, which had strengthened the office of the Librarian and required appointees to be confirmed. Young established a new professionalism at the Library, hiring many key future leaders. He died in office on January 17, 1899.

Herbert Putnam (1899–1939)
At the urging of the ALA, President McKinley appointed Putnam, librarian of the Boston Public Library and ALA president-elect, as Librarian on March 13, 1899. Putnam, the first experienced librarian to direct the Library of Congress, made American libraries a new and important constituency for the Nation's Library. In 1938, Putnam tendered his resignation to President Franklin D. Roosevelt but agreed to stay on as Librarian until a successor was found. Putnam assumed the office of Librarian Emeritus on October 1, 1939, the day before his successor assumed his duties.

Archibald MacLeish (1939–1944)
On May 11, 1939, President Roosevelt endorsed Supreme Court Justice Felix Frankfurter's suggestion that poet, writer, and lawyer

MacLeish, "a scholarly man of letters," would make a good
Librarian of Congress because the Library "is not merely a library."
MacLeish's nomination proved controversial. Although some
opposed his appointment because they believed he had pro-
Communist leanings and others because he was not "the ablest
library administrator available," the Senate ultimately confirmed
the nomination. MacLeish resigned on December 19, 1944, to
become assistant secretary of state.

Luther H. Evans (1945–1953)

President Roosevelt died on April 12, 1945, without having nominated MacLeish's successor. On June 18, 1945, President Harry
Truman nominated Chief Assistant Librarian of Congress Evans,
a political scientist and an experienced library administrator, to be
Librarian. Evans took the oath of office on June 30, 1945. He
resigned his position in July 1953, when he was elected director-
general of the United Nations Educational, Scientific and Cultural
Organization (UNESCO).

L. Quincy Mumford (1954–1974)

On April 22, 1954, President Dwight D. Eisenhower nominated
Mumford, director of the Cleveland Public Library and president-
elect of the American Library Association, to be Librarian. Mumford
became the first Librarian of Congress to have graduated from a
library school (B.S. degree in library science, Columbia University,
1929). He retired on December 31, 1974.

Daniel J. Boorstin (1975–1987)

On June 30, 1975, President Gerald R. Ford nominated author
and historian Boorstin, senior historian and former director of the
National Museum of History and Technology, Smithsonian
Institution, to be Librarian. Boorstin took the oath of office on
November 12, 1975. After retiring in 1987 to devote more time to
writing and lecturing, he became Librarian of Congress Emeritus
on August 4, 1987.

James H. Billington (1987–)

President Ronald Reagan nominated historian Billington,
director of the Woodrow Wilson International Center for Scholars
at the Smithsonian Institution, to be Librarian on April 17, 1987.
Billington took the oath of office in the Library's Great Hall on
September 14, 1987.

Appendix III

Consultants in Poetry/Poets Laureate

Far from being simply a storehouse of knowledge, the Library of Congress is active in the cultural life of the United States. It is not only a center for musical performances, but also a forum for readings, conferences, and symposia devoted to the majesty and music of the artfully spoken and written word. Poetry has been central to the Library's literary programs since Librarian of Congress Herbert Putnam named the first Consultant in Poetry to the Library of Congress to help him strengthen and exploit the Library's poetry collections. Some of the greatest figures in American literature have served as Consultant in Poetry. In 1986 that title was expanded, with congressional approval, to Poet Laureate, Consultant in Poetry to reflect the importance of this post to the literary life of the nation.

Consultants in Poetry

Joseph Auslander	1937–1941
Allen Tate	1943–1944
Robert Penn Warren	1944–1945
Louise Bogan	1945–1946
Karl Shapiro	1946–1947
Robert Lowell	1947–1948
Leonie Adams	1948–1949
Elizabeth Bishop	1949–1950
Conrad Aiken	1950–1952
William Carlos Williams	*(appointed in 1952 but did not serve)*
Randall Jarrell	1956–1958
Robert Frost	1958–1959
Richard Eberhart	1959–1961
Louis Untermeyer	1961–1963
Howard Nemerov	1963–1964
Reed Whittemore	1964–1965
Stephen Spender	1965–1966
James Dickey	1966–1968
William Jay Smith	1968–1970
William Stafford	1970–1971
Josephine Jacobsen	1971–1973
Daniel Hoffman	1973–1974
Stanley Kunitz	1974–1976
Robert Hayden	1976–1978
William Meredith	1978–1980
Maxine Kumin	1980–1982
Anthony Hecht	1982–1984
Robert Fitzgerald	1984–1985

| Reed Whittemore | *(Interim Consultant in Poetry, 1984–1985)* |
| Gwendolyn Brooks | 1985–1986 |

Poet Laureate, Consultants in Poetry

Robert Penn Warren	1986–1987
Richard Wilbur	1987–1988
Howard Nemerov	1988–1990
Mark Strand	1990–1991
Joseph Brodsky	1991–1992
Mona Van Duyn	1992–1993
Rita Dove	1993–1995
Robert Hass	1995–1997
Robert Pinsky	1997–2000
Rita Dove	*(Special Bicentennial Consultant 1999–2000)*
Louise Glück	*(Special Bicentennial Consultant 1999–2000)*
W.S. Merwin	*(Special Bicentennial Consultant 1999–2000)*
Stanley Kunitz	2000–2001
Billy Collins	2001–2003
Louise Glück	2003–2004
Ted Kooser	2004–2006
Donald Hall	2006–2007
Charles Simic	2007–2008
Kay Ryan	2008–2010
W. S. Merwin	2010–2011
Philip Levine	2011–

Appendix IV

Read More About the Library of Congress and its Collections

American Treasures in the Library of Congress, introduction by Garry Wills. NY: Harry N. Abrams, 1997.

America's Library: The Story of the Library of Congress, by James Conaway. New Haven, CT: Yale University Press, 2000.

Encyclopedia of the Library of Congress: For Congress, the Nation & the World, edited by John Y. Cole and Jane Aikin. Lanham, MD: Bernan Press, 2004.

For Congress and the Nation: A Chronological History of the Library of Congress, by John Y. Cole. Washington, D.C.: Library of Congress, 1979.

Full Circle: Ninety Years of Service in the Main Reading Room, by Josephus Nelson and Judith Farley. Washington, D.C.: Library of Congress, 1991.

Jefferson's Legacy: A Brief History of the Library of Congress, by John Y. Cole. Washington, D.C.: Library of Congress, 1993.

The Library of Congress: An Architectural Alphabet. London: Scala Publishers Ltd., 2011.

The Library of Congress: The Art and Architecture of the Thomas Jefferson Building, edited by John Y. Cole and Henry Hope Reed. NY: Norton, 1997.

On These Walls: Inscriptions and Quotations in the Library of Congress, by John Y. Cole, with photographs by Carol M. Highsmith. London: Scala Publishers, 2008.

Illustrated Guides to the Collections of the Library of Congress

Library of Congress African and Middle Eastern Collections: Illustrated Guides, by Joanne M. Zellers, Levon Avdoyan, and Michael W. Grunberger. Boxed, 3-volume set. Washington, D.C.: Library of Congress, 2001.

Library of Congress Asian Collections: An Illustrated Guide, by Harold E. Meinheit, with an introduction by Mya Thanda Poe. Washington, D.C.: Library of Congress, 2000.

Library of Congress European Collections: An Illustrated Guide, with an introduction by Michael H. Haltzel. Washington, D.C.: Library of Congress, 1995.

Library of Congress Geography and Maps: An Illustrated Guide, introduction by Ralph E. Ehrenberg. Washington, D.C.: Library of Congress, 1996.

Library of Congress Hispanic and Portuguese Collections: An Illustrated Guide, with an introduction by John R. Hébert. Washington, D.C.: Library of Congress, 1996.

Library of Congress Folklife Center: An Illustrated Guide, by James
   Hardin, foreword by Peggy A. Bulger. Includes a compact disc
   with audio recordings. Washington, D.C.: Library of Congress,
   2004.

Library of Congress Law Library: An Illustrated Guide, by Jolande
   Goldberg and Natalie Gawdiak. Washington, D.C.: Library of
   Congress, 2005.

Library of Congress Manuscripts: An Illustrated Guide, introduction by
   James H. Hutson. Washington, D.C.: Library of Congress, 1993.

*Library of Congress Motion Pictures, Broadcasting, Recorded Sound:
   An Illustrated Guide*, introduction by David Francis. Washington,
   D.C.: Library of Congress, 2002.

Library of Congress Music, Theater, Dance: An Illustrated Guide,
   introduction by James W. Pruett. Washington, D.C.: Library of
   Congress, 1993.

Library of Congress Prints and Photographs: An Illustrated Guide, by
   Bernard F. Reilly Jr., and curators of the Prints and Photographs
   Division; preface by Stephen E. Ostrow. Washington, D.C.:
   Library of Congress, 1995.

Library of Congress Resource Guides

*The African-American Mosaic: A Library of Congress Resource Guide
   for the Study of Black History and Culture*, edited by Debra
   Newman Ham. Washington, D.C.: Library of Congress, 1993.

The African American Odyssey, edited by Debra Newman Ham.
   Washington, D.C.: Library of Congress, 1998.

*American Women: A Library of Congress Guide for the Study of
   Women's History and Culture in the United States*, edited by
   Sheridan Harvey, Janice E. Ruth, Barbara Natanson, Sara Day,
   and Evelyn Sinclair. Washington, D.C.: Library of Congress,
   2001.

*Many Nations: A Library of Congress Resource Guide for the Study of
   Indian and Alaska Native Peoples of the United States*, edited by
   Patrick Frazier and the Publishing Office. Washington, D.C.:
   Library of Congress, 1996.

Information About Images

To order reproductions of images in this book: Note the Library of Congress negative number provided on this page (numbers beginning with LC-USZ62 indicate black and white images and those beginning with LC-USZC4 indicate color images, digital files begin with LC-DIG). Where no negative number exists, note, in the image's caption, the Library division and the title of the item. Duplicates may be ordered from the Library of Congress' Duplication Services:
Website: http://www.loc.gov/duplicationservices/
Mailing address: Library of Congress, Duplication Services,
 101 Independence Avenue S.E., Washington, DC 20540-4570
Phone: (202) 707-5640
Fax: (202) 707-1771
E-mail: duplicationservices@loc.gov

Services to Congress and Libraries

Public Programs and Services

Children's Literature Center

Concerts, Broadcasts, and Film Showings

Office of Scholarly Programs

Preserving the Past, Informing the Future: The Library of Congress in the Digital Age

Back Matter

A photographic or digital copy of this 1906 stereo slide of the Taj Mahal (Prints and Photographs Division) can be acquired from LC Duplication Services by citing its Library of Congress negative number (LC-USZ62-113606).

Index

Figures in **bold** refer to illustrations.

Schematic Diagram
of the Thomas Jefferson
Building

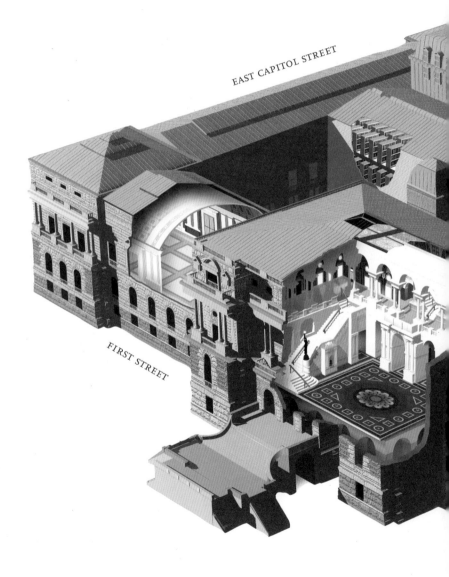

EAST CAPITOL STREET

FIRST STREET